Main Meal Salads

Main Meal Salads

NORMAN KOLPAS

Photographs by

MICHAEL GRAND

Reader's Digest

Published by The Reader's Digest Association Limited
London • New York • Sydney • Cape Town • Montreal

A READER'S DIGEST BOOK

Published by The Reader's Digest Association Limited
11 Westferry Circus
Canary Wharf
London E14 4HE

ISBN 0 276 42355 0

A CIP data record for this book is available from the British Library.

This book was designed and produced by
Michael Friedman Publishing Group, Inc.
15 West 26th Street
New York, New York 10010
USA

Editor: Nathaniel Marunas
Designer: Andrea Karman
Design Layout: Lynne Yeamans
Photography Editor: Christopher C. Bain
Production Director: Karen Matsu Greenberg
Prop sourcing and styling: Leslie Defrancesco
Food preparation and styling: Jennifer Udel

Color separations by Colourscan Overseas Co Pte Ltd
Printed in England by Butler & Tanner Limited

C O N T E N T S

Introduction

Oh herbaceous treat!
'Twould tempt the dying anchorite to eat;
Back to the world he'd turn his fleeting soul,
And plunge his fingers in the salad bowl;
Serenely full, the epicure would say
'Fate cannot harm me—I have dined today.'

—Sydney Smith, 'Recipe for Salad' (1843)

Never have the lines penned by the nineteenth-century essayist Sydney Smith seemed more prophetic. A glance at any good restaurant's menu today will tell you that we live in an era when the salad has truly come of age, having been elevated to the status of fine dining experience.

This book celebrates main meal salads in all their diversity. It begins with an overview of the elements that go into making such salads, from a guide to salad-making equipment to a glossary of salad leaves and all the various items that might top them or be tossed with them, including instructions for roasting peppers, peeling and seeding tomatoes, toasting nuts, and making croûtons and other crisp bread accompaniments. Following these basics comes an overview of the various elements that make up salad dressings, including recipes for some classic mixtures.

These fundamentals are followed by 60 main meal salad recipes, photographed expressly for this book by Michael Grand and divided into themes: Classics and Variations, Chopped Salads, Robust Salads, and Light and Refreshing Salads. The book concludes with a guide to mail-order ingredients suppliers.

It is my sincerest hope that you will like the recipes so much that they become standards in your home repertoire, that they will introduce you to a new way of eating meals that are healthy and that refresh and revive your body and spirit even as they satisfy.

—*Norman Kolpas*

Equipment

Most salads are very easy to make and require little if any special equipment. There are, however, a few basic kitchen tools used in making salads, an understanding of which will help you achieve even better results.

Your Hands

I can still remember my astonishment when, as a London-based writer assigned in the mid-1970s to the legendary cooking series *The Good Cook*, I first witnessed renowned cook and series consultant Richard Olney plunge his bare hands deep into a bowl to toss a salad. The gesture seemed downright pagan, a far cry from the fastidious cooking habits of my mother. I loved it.

Olney taught all of us on the series that the best kitchen tools you have are your own hands. Nothing else comes as close to letting you judge textures, temperatures and the degree to which things are blended.

While I wouldn't dream of suggesting that anyone using this book present a beautiful salad to guests at the table and then bury their hands deep within it, do give it a try when you're hidden away in the kitchen. Nor should you forget how useful your hands are for tearing salad greens into bite-size chunks, an essential task that yields results a knife cannot match.

When working with these least expensive, most invaluable kitchen tools, don't worry that they're somehow unhygienic: well-washed hands are at least as clean as well-washed mixing spoons. Once you get over any residual squeamishness, you might just discover a new form of fun.

Knives

Good kitchen knives are essential for slicing salad vegetables, carving meat and poultry toppings and a wide range of other tasks. Yet I am constantly surprised by how *so* many people who aspire to become good cooks try to make do with less-than-good, less-than-sharp knives.

You should seek out a basic set of good quality knives with sharp, sturdy stainless steel blades and with handles that are securely attached and that feel perfectly comfortable in your hand. For salads, you'll need at the very least a small paring knife, for cutting up small items, for peeling and—yes—paring and for small, detail-oriented tasks like cutting the cores out of tomatoes; and a so-called chef's knife, which is a medium-size slicing and chopping blade about 20cm (8in) long. I'm also fond of my long, serrated bread/carving knife, which is useful for slicing steak or chicken breast toppings, although you could also use a good, sharp chef's knife for the task.

On the topic of sharpness, another sobering piece of advice needs to be added. Yes, you must be careful around sharp knives and store them safely in a place—most likely a wooden knife block—that not only protects their sharp edges but also protects you, your family and any guests in your kitchen. But you *must* keep those knives sharp. Most home knife-sharpening tools, I find, don't do the trick. We periodically have ours professionally sharpened, either at a knife shop or at a local butcher's shop. Remember, too, that a dull knife is far more dangerous than a sharp knife as it is more likely to slip during cutting.

Cutting Boards

A good kitchen knife is good for nothing without a proper cutting surface. The best choices for cutting boards boil down to two: traditional wooden boards or blocks and acrylic cutting boards.

In my own kitchen, I use the latter type. Most kitchen shops stock several different makes. Look for those that have some give or texture to them, rather than being hard and slick, so that both the knife and the food you are cutting will be less likely to slip.

I keep reading conflicting studies on whether wood or acrylic is supposed to be more hygienic—that is, less likely to harbour bacteria from the foods you prepare. I've even seen some acrylic boards that have bactericidal substances embedded in them. My own practice is, when preparing a recipe that contains both meat (or poultry or seafood) and vegetables requiring cutting, to use one board exclusively for the vegetables and the other exclusively for the raw meat; to further avoid cross-contamination, I tend to use separate knives with each cutting board. Needless to say, good scrubbing with lots of hot soapy water goes a long way towards maintaining good kitchen hygiene.

Other Cutting Tools

A wide variety of other kitchen cutting tools can be useful when preparing salads. Among them are vegetable peelers, of which I find the swivel-bladed variety the most efficient; citrus zesters, small tools with sharp-edged holes that remove citrus zest in thin little strips; and, most important, a handheld box grater/shredder, which you can use to quickly grate citrus zest or a hard cheese like Parmesan, or grate anything from a carrot to a block of Cheddar cheese.

Grill Pans

A number of the recipes in this book call for the featured topping for a salad to be grilled or barbecued. I want here to offer one more option, the grill pan, which is widely available and which offers both the convenience of grilling and much of the appealing results of barbecuing.

Grill pans are a type of frying pan, usually made of cast-iron or heavy-gauge aluminium, which have raised parallel ridges across their surface. Often these ridged surfaces are also treated to be non-stick. Heated on top of your cooker, they build up an intense heat that can sear-cook steak, chicken breasts or seafood, cooking them quickly while endowing

them with the kind of char marks you usually only get from a barbecue.

You'll find such grill pans in well-stocked, high-quality kitchen equipment shops and department stores. They are well worth seeking out, and can certainly be used with ease to cook any of the grilled salad toppings on these pages.

Salad Spinners

In my time, I've owned several salad spinners, those devices that hold just-washed salad leaves in a slotted basket that is made to spin by hand-crank or pulley, and thus fling all the water off the leaves into the outer container. Mine always seem to wear out, though—maybe because they're so much fun to play with. (When my son, Jacob, was a toddler, he played with one incessantly until it wouldn't spin anymore.)

By all means get one if you like. In fact, seek out an old-fashioned French salad spinner, a wire basket in which you enclose the leaves and then, grasping the basket by its handle, step out into the garden and spin it round and round at the end of your swinging arm.

Just the same, most salad leaves will dry out just fine if you spread them out on absorbent tea towels and then loosely roll them up. (See also my suggestions on pages 14–15 for storing and crisping salad leaves in the refrigerator.)

Mixing Bowls

Salad making, it seems to me, demands more mixing bowls than just about any other type of cooking: bowls in which to mix dressings, bowls in which to marinate featured ingredients, bowls to hold separate elements of a salad before you assemble the final presentation, bowls in which to toss and mix all the ingredients together.

When buying your bowls, look for items made of sturdy heavy glassware, glazed earthenware or ceramic, none of which is likely to react with acidic ingredients.

When selecting the size bowl you'll need for any task, first estimate all the measured-out ingredients that you'll be putting into or combining in the bowl. Then select a bowl of a size that looks like it will comfortably hold those ingredients. Finally, put that bowl aside and pick the next largest size. That's my own time-tested strategy for ensuring that you'll always have enough room to mix things properly.

This brings me to the topic of large salad bowls. Many of the salads in this book call for as much as 900g (2lb) of salad leaves alone to serve four people. That quantity translates to a 4 litre (7 pint) capacity bowl, and, allowing for other ingredients and room to toss things thoroughly, it really demands a bowl twice the size—or that you prepare the salad in separate batches.

Most nesting bowl sets don't come with that large a bowl, so you'll have to buy a big salad bowl as well. A good place to look for inexpensive ones, I've found, is at a professional restaurant supply or catering shop, where you'll find giant hemispherical bowls made of plastic, aluminium or stainless steel—perfectly utilitarian tools that you can use to mix up a giant salad.

Salad Servers

If I remember correctly after all these years, my wife and I got amongst our wedding presents at least three different sets of salad servers—you know, those long, giant fork-and-spoon pairs that everyone insists you need to toss and serve a salad. Whenever I can tactfully do so, I avoid using them (see my previous comments on hands as kitchen tools). However, I still do occasionally break them out when the need arises to toss and serve a salad at the table.

I can't make any recommendation about design. There are so many different 'salad sets'—big salad bowls, serving bowls and servers, all wrapped up together as a gift. They're all very stylish, so choosing a design is really a matter of taste. I do have stronger feelings, though, about material. Smooth plastic, acrylic or metal servers, I find, are too slippery, easily losing their grip on salad leaves that have been coated with dressing. Wood, for me, is a much better choice of material, having enough of a textured surface to really grasp the ingredients of a salad, no matter how slippery, and thus making tossing easier.

Serving Plates and Bowls

Main meal salads call for big dinner-size plates or bowls rather than the more demure containers normally used for salads. At a minimum, the salads in this book require plates about 25cm (10in) in diameter and, for those with a lot of leaves and other ingredients, deep bowls of about the same width. I also find myself frequently serving salads in Italian-style pasta bowls, wide shallow containers about 5–7.5cm (2–3in) deep.

The most important piece of advice I can give you on choosing your serving plates and bowls, though, is to use your imagination. Just as most of the recipes in this book break the conventional boundaries of the salad world, so too should you feel absolutely free to break from convention and serve your creations in whatever containers come to hand, work sufficiently well for the given recipe, and help make your presentation as attractive as possible.

CHAPTER 1

A Guide to Salad Ingredients

Although relatively easy to prepare, main meal salads are, by their very nature, more complex constructions than their familiar starters or side-dish cousins. Each element of a main meal salad plays a particular role, its tastes, textures, shapes and colours dynamically interplaying with the other parts of the salad. The following guide should give you a good idea of how this give-and-take amongst ingredients works, while introducing you to the basic elements of the main meal salad.

Salad Leaves

The leaves you use—and I say 'leaves' rather than the more popular words 'greens' or 'lettuces' to reflect the wider variety of choices available to cooks today—go a long way towards determining the personality of the salad you make.

Despite the incredible variety of leaves available today to most cooks, you'll notice that in most of the recipes in this book I suggest only *types* of leaves, such as bitter greens, or call for generic blends, such as mixed baby salad leaves. When I make a specific recommendation, it is for leaves that are likely to be available in most supermarkets, such as cos or round lettuce; in my Test Kitchen Notes, I suggest other options if you are unable to find the kinds of leaves mentioned in the ingredients list.

CHICORY

Small, slender cylindrical heads of crisp-tender, spear-shaped leaves prized for their refreshing, slightly bitter taste. Smaller, paler-coloured heads, tending towards white and a yellow-green rather than darker shades of green, have a subtler, more pleasant flavour. Good with fairly strong-tasting toppings or mixed with other leaves.

CHARD
(also called Swiss Chard)

Chard has vibrant green leaves and broad white or red stems. Leaves should be springy to the touch, stems in a compact bunch, the bases connected to each other at the bottom. Slightly bitter in flavour, this vitamin-rich green can be used like spinach in combination with other leaves or with strong-tasting ingredients.

ROCKET

Fairly strong-tasting, pleasantly bitter and slightly peppery leaves, resembling spinach in their deep green colour and relatively tender texture. Good on their own as a background for robust ingredients, or mixed with milder leaves.

ROUND LETTUCE
(also called Butterhead)

Very tender, small, frilly leaves with a pale green colour and a delicate, mild taste. Best as a background for more subtly flavoured ingredients or those with delicate texture.

ICEBERG LETTUCE

A classic cool, crisp favourite, with a mild, unassertive flavour. The pale green leaves make attractive 'cups' for lining serving plates.

MINI CHINESE LEAF

Very mild-tasting variety of cabbage with long leaves composed of crisp white ribs and very crinkly leaves. Excellent in Asian-style salads.

RED CABBAGE

Tightly packed, deep purple leaves with an assertive flavour and crisp texture that may be moderated by shredding and briefly dousing with boiling water. A standby in slaw-type salads.

COS

Very crisp lettuce whose long, ribbed leaves have a distinctive but not assertive flavour; inner leaves taste milder and have a softer texture.

RADICCHIO

Smallish heads of bright, deep purplish-red leaves with white ribs, a moderately crisp, cabbage-like texture and, particularly in smaller leaves, a pleasant, bracingly bitter taste that complements strong-flavoured ingredients. Radicchio is often included in salad leaf mixtures for its colour.

RED-LEAF LETTUCE

Tender, fairly large, loose leaves with a mild taste that belies its assertive appearance.

CHINESE LEAF

Medium-green cabbage whose leaves have a moderate flavour and a very crinkly appearance that lends itself to attractive presentations.

SPINACH

Pleasantly earthy-tasting, tender leaves that lend themselves very well to robust-flavoured salads. Larger leaves can tend towards a tougher texture and stronger flavour, as well as having stringy ribs, and they require tearing into bite-size pieces. Baby spinach leaves are prized for their milder taste, tenderness and highly attractive appearance.

WATERCRESS

Peppery-tasting, refreshingly cool and crisp sprigs of dark green little leaves that nicely complement rich or strong-tasting ingredients.

Mixed Baby Salad Leaves

Immature forms of many of the leaves mentioned here, along with other, more esoteric leaves and herbs, are being widely marketed today as mixed baby salad leaves, sold in supermarkets already washed, dried, bagged and labelled. The culinary advantages of such mixtures lie in their freshness of flavour, their tenderness, the variety of subtle tastes and textures they present, and the beautiful presentations they offer. For the busy cook, they also offer the advantage of ease—just grab a filled bag and you have the foundation of a main meal salad right in your hand.

With such quality and ease in mind, many of the recipes in this book call for such leaves. However, if the supermarkets you frequent do not offer them, buy instead the smallest, tenderest specimens of whatever variety of salad leaves are available to you, even if that amounts to only one or two types. And if you can't get true baby leaves, simply buy the smallest ones on display and select the smaller, inner leaves; or tear larger leaves into bite-size pieces.

Again, use such mixtures if they are convenient for you. If they aren't, never let their lack of availability keep you from enjoying any main course salad in this book.

Selecting and Preparing Salad Leaves

Vegetables of all kinds, including salad leaves, are fresher, cleaner and more ready to be eaten today than they ever were in the past. That doesn't mean, however, that you should skimp on the attention you pay to preparing the leaves you buy for the table.

When shopping for salad leaves, seek out those that are bright and fresh-looking, well-formed and free of blemishes. Don't get hung up on dirt, which can be washed off at home; look past it to the quality of the leaves themselves. Avoid anything that appears to be drooping or has any brown spots. When selecting prepackaged leaves, check to see if there is a use-by date, then look through the clear parts on the wrapper, applying the same criteria as above and paying special attention to detect any rotting leaves.

Once at home, store leaves in the crisper drawer of your refrigerator and use within a day or two if you can; of course, the leaves will last longer, but they will diminish in texture and flavour.

Don't wash leaves until shortly before use, because any water left clinging to them for too long can hasten their decline. Except for very hard, tightly packed cabbages and the like, separate leaves by hand rather than with a knife, to avoid damaging or bruising them.

Rinse off any dirt under cold running water, except in the case of spinach, which grows in very sandy soil and is prone to hold on to its dirt. For spinach, fill a sink or bowl with cold water, then immerse the leaves in it and slosh them round. Next, lift the leaves out of the water and set them aside, then drain the sink or bowl and rinse out the sand that will have settled on the bottom. Repeat the procedure until the spinach leaves no residue of sand when lifted out.

After leaves are washed, dry them in a salad spinner (see page 8) or by patting them between clean tea towels or double thicknesses of kitchen paper towel. Then gently roll up the leaves in the towels to keep in the refrigerator until the time comes to assemble the salad.

Do not cut or tear leaves until just before serving time. Cutting is necessary for hardy leaves like those of cabbage, or when particularly fine-textured effects are desired, as for slaws or chopped salads. In all other cases, simply tear the salad leaves into bite-size pieces with your fingers. The results will be more pleasingly varied than uniformly cut leaves, and they will be less subject to unsightly bruising and discoloration.

Other Vegetables

A cornucopia of other vegetables make appearances in main meal salads. The following entries highlight some of the more common choices. Particulars on more unusual or less frequently used ingredients can be found in the Test Kitchen Notes of individual recipes in which they appear.

THE ONION FAMILY

Various kinds of onions and their cousins give sharp, biting flavour and crisp, crunchy texture to main meal salads. Most often, they are used to highlight other ingredients rather than call attention to themselves. For that reason, I tend to shy away from using garlic in main meal salads, with the exception of its indispensability in various kinds of Caesar salad (see pages 30–36). When I want a fairly pungent effect, I opt instead for shallots, whose flavour tends to hover midway between that of garlic and onion. My favourite kind of salad onions are sweet white varieties that, though offering good onion flavour, also possess a distinctive overlay of sugary mildness, with none of the harshness of other onions. If you can't find these, red onions are a good alternative.

PEPPERS

The mild, vaguely bell-shaped members of the pepper family, also known as capsicums, have an important role in salads both in their raw form and roasted (see recipe right). Raw peppers have a wonderfully juicy crispness and a nice, sharp bite of flavour that grows mellower and sweeter as the peppers ripen from their green state to various shades of red (the most common ripened form), yellow and orange. These different, bright hues also lend attractive colour to salads. To prepare raw peppers for salads, their tough stalks and indigestible seeds and spongy white internal membranes must first be removed. Use a sharp knife to cut a pepper in halves or quarters vertically through the stalk and flower end; then, with your fingers, pull out the stalk sections and the clusters of seeds attached to it, as well as any remaining seeds and ribs inside each piece. Cut up the pepper flesh as called for in the recipe. (Note that the same technique applies to preparing raw chillies for salads. Bear in mind, however, that you must exercise great caution when handling chillies, as their volatile oils can burn your skin, any cuts or abrasions, or your eyes. If your hands are particularly sensitive, wear rubber gloves when preparing chillies. Wash your hands with lots of warm soapy water, and do not touch your eyes or other sensitive areas.)

When roasted until their shiny skins blister and blacken, peppers develop a wonderful sweetness and become tender and juicy, making a wonderful embellishment for many main meal salads. If you are in a rush to use such peppers in a salad, keep on hand jars of roasted peppers, packed in salted water or in oil (often sold in supermarkets or in Italian delicatessens). For the absolute best flavour and texture, however, roast the peppers yourself.

To roast peppers, preheat the grill. Place the peppers on a foil-lined baking sheet or dish beneath the grill and cook them, turning occasionally, until their skins are evenly blackened and blistered, 10 to 15 minutes. Remove them from the grill and cover them with another sheet of foil, leaving them at room temperature until they are cool enough to handle. Then, with your fingers, peel off the blistered skins; tear or cut open the peppers, taking special care in case any steam lingers inside them, and remove and discard the stalks, membranes and seeds, using a small spoon if necessary to pick up any errant seeds. As a bonus, save the juices that run from the peppers. They have a sweet flavour that can enhance a salad dressing.

FRESH TOMATOES

Especially in summer, when vine-ripened varieties appear in supermarkets and offer cooks the best in firm, juicy-crisp texture and intensely sweet-savoury flavour, tomatoes are a significant part of main meal salads. Shun, however, most hothouse varieties, which tend to be mushy and flavourless. For the best all-round tomato at any time of year, seek out the small, cylindrical variety known as Italian or plum tomatoes. Tomatoes should never be refrigerated as they lose their flavour and texture as a result of the cold; instead, leave unused tomatoes in the open or in a paper bag in the kitchen so that their delicious flavour and meaty texture are maintained.

The peels and seeds of tomatoes offer nothing to salads, being indigestible and flavourless. However, for the most part there is no need to remove them, except for the most fastidious of presentations or for those salads whose appearance, taste or texture might be lessened by the watery matter that surrounds tomato seeds.

To peel tomatoes, bring a saucepan of water to the boil and, on the work surface nearby, set a mixing bowl full of ice and water. Use the tip of a small, sharp knife to cut out the cores of the tomatoes, then score a shallow X in the opposite flower ends. With a slotted spoon, lower the tomatoes into the boiling water, immersing them completely for about 20 seconds to loosen their skins, then transfer them to the iced water to chill. Using your fingers or the knife, peel off the skins. Then cut the tomatoes crossways in half and, with your fingertips or the handle of a teaspoon, scoop out the seed sacs from each half (of course, you can seed an uncooked tomato in the same fashion).

Pasta

All kinds of pasta can add hearty flavour and chewy texture to salads, whether they embellish a main meal mixture or replace most of the salad greens in one of the main-meal pasta salads you'll find scattered throughout this book. You'll find specifics on different types of pasta—including Asian noodles—in the Test Kitchen Notes of individual recipes. Take care to cook pasta for salads only until tender but still chewy, what the Italians call *al dente*, or 'to the bite'. This is because the pasta will soak up some of the dressing and continue to soften slightly; so *al dente* cooking will ensure perfectly textured, non-mushy pasta in your salad.

Cheese

For many people, a main meal salad simply does not qualify unless it includes the richness and, sometimes, the tang of good cheese. You'll find fairly common cheeses such as Cheddar, Gruyère, blue and Parmesan used in various recipes throughout this book. Less familiar to some will be the fresh, creamy goat's milk cheese I sometimes call for, available in well-stocked supermarkets and specialist cheese shops.

Red Meat

One of the marvellous things about a main meal salad is the way it enables you to stretch a little red meat a long way, one of the tenets of the health-conscious contemporary diet. When recipes in this book call for steak, lamb or pork, you'll find that the quantity divides up to no more than about 115g (4oz) per serving. Yet you get to enjoy the meat's rich savour, backed up and complemented by a wide variety of vegetables. Because meat stars in some of the most elegant main meal salads in this book, you will want to seek out the best supplier available for well trimmed, high quality meats.

Poultry

Poultry in main meal salads means white-meat chicken, one of the healthiest choices for protein available today. The recipes in this book take advantage of the widespread availability and convenience of ready-to-cook boneless, skinless chicken breasts. Still other salads in this book utilise left-over chicken, making them ideal choices for lunch or a light dinner on the day after you have roasted a whole bird.

Seafood

Grilled seafood fillets such as salmon or tuna, or freshly grilled prawns or scallops, are especially pleasurable toppings for light and flavourful main meal salads. Seek out a fishmonger, whether in a supermarket, shop or stall, who offers you a good choice of fresh, high quality seafood, and never buy anything that doesn't look clear, moist and fresh, and have any aroma about it other than the fresh, clean scent of the sea. A good fishmonger will also have available two of the most convenient items for main meal seafood salads: freshly cooked crabmeat and cooked prawns.

Nuts and Seeds

Nuts of all kinds—including peanuts, almonds, walnuts, pecans, hazelnuts, macadamias and pine nuts—add crunch and savour to salads, as do toasted sesame seeds. Toasting makes them all the crunchier and richer (and enables you to remove the skins of hazelnuts).

Toasted Nuts and Sesame Seeds

1. Preheat the oven to 160°C (325°F, gas mark 3).

2. Spread the nuts or sesame seeds in a single layer on a foil-lined baking sheet or baking dish. Bake the nuts just until they are light golden brown, turning them occasionally with a wooden spoon and checking frequently to guard against scorching. Roasting time will depend on size: sesame seeds will need no more than about 1 minute, pine nuts or flaked almonds 3 to 5 minutes, whole nuts up to 10 minutes. The residual heat in the nuts will continue to darken them slightly after removal from the oven.

3. After roasting hazelnuts, fold them inside a tea towel and rub vigorously to loosen their skins. After they have cooled, use your fingertips to remove any residual bits of skin, but don't bother to remove any pieces that remain clinging tightly.

Breads

No salad meal is complete without a crusty loaf of bread, ready to complement the food, cleanse the palate between bites, and sop up the last traces of dressing and juices once the salad is gone. I am an avid exponent of the excellent bakeries that seem to be popping up everywhere—a trend that happily shows no signs of abating. Indeed, many supermarkets nowadays bake all kinds of breads on the premises. Have a field day choosing one or more types of special breads that you feel will best complement the main meal salads you plan to prepare.

Bread, of course, also plays a more integral role in main meal salads in the form of croûtons, crostini and toasts. The following recipes offer some classic basics and variations called for in several of the salad recipes in this book. Use a firm-textured white or sourdough country-style loaf, such as an Italian *filone* or French *flûte* or *baguette*, preferably purchased from a quality bakery. For the best results, the bread should be a day or two old so that its crumb will have firmed up and dried out sufficiently for you to cut it into cubes that will toast up well. If you want to use up a whole loaf, you can double or triple the recipe and store the toasts in an airtight container for several days.

Croûtons

MAKES ABOUT 115g (4oz)

4 slices country-style white bread, cut
   1cm (½in) thick
6 tablespoons extra virgin olive oil or
   melted unsalted butter

1. Preheat the oven to 180°C (350°F,
gas mark 4).

2. With a sharp knife, cut the bread
slices into 1cm (½in) cubes (trim off the
crusts only if you want to). Put the
cubes in a mixing bowl and, tossing
them continuously but gently, drizzle in
the oil or butter to coat them evenly.

3. Spread the cubes in a single layer
on a baking sheet and bake, turning
them once or twice, until evenly golden
brown, about 15 minutes. Leave to cool
at room temperature, then store in an
airtight container until ready to use.

Variations

GARLIC CROÛTONS

With a garlic press, squeeze 1 or 2
peeled garlic cloves into a small bowl
and stir together with the oil or butter
before mixing with the bread cubes.

GARLIC SPICE CROÛTONS

Along with the garlic above, stir in a
pinch of pure ground red chilli powder
or paprika with the oil or butter.

LEMON GARLIC CROÛTONS

Along with the garlic above, stir in
1 tablespoon finely grated lemon zest
with the oil or butter.

GARLIC PARMESAN CROÛTONS

Along with the garlic above, stir in
2 tablespoons freshly grated Parmesan
cheese with the oil or butter.

FAT-FREE GARLIC CROÛTONS

Before cutting the bread slices into
cubes, use a garlic press to purée 1 or 2
garlic cloves and spread the garlic all
over both sides of each slice.

TEST KITCHEN NOTES

THE CRISPLY TOASTED CUBES OF BREAD
KNOWN AS CROÛTONS ADD RICH CRUNCH
AND SAVOUR TO SALADS, AS WELL AS THE
SPARK OF WHATEVER SEASONINGS YOU
MIGHT ADD TO THE CROÛTONS (SEE
ACCOMPANYING VARIATIONS). THE ESSEN-
TIAL ELEMENT, OF COURSE, IS GOOD BREAD.

USE YOUR CHOICE OF OLIVE OIL OR
BUTTER, OR A BLEND.

Crostini

175ml (6fl oz) extra virgin olive oil
24 diagonal slices cut 5mm (¼in) thick
    from a long, narrow white bread loaf

1. Preheat the oven to 190°C (375°F, gas mark 5).

2. Dipping a pastry brush repeatedly into the olive oil, evenly brush both sides of each bread slice with the oil. Place the slices on a foil-lined baking sheet.

3. Bake until the toasts are crisp and golden brown, about 6 minutes on each side. Serve immediately.

TEST KITCHEN NOTES

THESE ITALIAN-STYLE BREAD TOASTS MAY BE TUCKED INTO THE SIDES OF SALADS OR SERVED IN PLACE OF BREAD.

Parmesan Toasts

175g (6oz) unsalted butter, softened
115g (4oz) Parmesan cheese, freshly grated
24 diagonal slices cut 5mm (¼in) thick
    from a long, narrow white bread loaf

1. Preheat the oven to 190°C (375°F, gas mark 5).

2. In a shallow bowl, use a fork to mash together the butter and cheese. With a table knife, generously spread the butter and cheese mixture on to one side of each bread slice. Place the slices buttered sides up on a foil-lined baking sheet.

3. Bake until the bread and its topping are crisp and golden brown, about 12 minutes. Serve immediately.

Variations

GARLIC-PARMESAN TOASTS

With a garlic press, purée 1 or 2 garlic cloves into the mixing bowl, mashing them together with the butter and cheese.

GARLIC TOASTS

Omit the cheese and, with a garlic press, purée 1 or 2 garlic cloves into the mixing bowl, mashing them together with the butter.

TEST KITCHEN NOTES

THESE CRISP, SAVOURY TOASTS MAKE A NICE COMPLEMENT TO ROBUST SALADS, PILED ON TOP OF THE BED OF GREENS OR SERVED FROM A NAPKIN-LINED BASKET ON THE SIDE.

YOU CAN VARY THE RECIPE TO YOUR TASTE BY ADDING OTHER SEASONINGS, OR BY LEAVING OUT THE CHEESE (SEE ACCOMPANYING VARIATIONS).

CHAPTER 2

The Art of the Dressing

Dressing is the sauce of a main meal salad. Like any sauce, it contributes unique character through its taste and texture, while marrying all the salad's diverse ingredients by uniformly coating them.

Achieving the delicate balance between the leaves and the dressing is part of the art of dressing a salad. It is important to select the dressing's specific ingredients for their individual properties as well as how they suit your own tastes, a point that applies particularly to flavoured oils like olive oil (see pages 23–24). Actually adding the dressing and tossing the salad is the final part of the art.

On the topic of tossing salads, in the recipes in this book I simply tell you at what point to toss the salad. It is worth stressing here, however, that salads should be adequately dressed to your taste and well tossed. In my testing, I have striven to include ample dressing for each recipe, because I generally like salads that are generously dressed and think that most other people do as well. Because most of the recipes call for the dressing to be mixed and held separately until serving time, however, you have the option of adding only as much dressing as you like, or of passing dressing separately for guests to serve themselves.

As for tossing salads, there's an old Italian saying that salads should be tossed thirty-three times, once for each year of Jesus's life. Not that there's any deep spiritual connection to the tossing of a salad. I think that was just a vivid way to remind a religious people that salads should be tossed well. Don't shy away from the task. If you're tossing the salad in the kitchen, dare to plunge your (well-washed) hands into the salad bowl so you can turn over all the ingredients and mix them up thoroughly, feeling with your fingertips that precise moment when they are all well and truly coated with the dressing. Be careful not to toss the salad for so long that it bruises and becomes limp, and don't leave the greens in an acidic dressing for too long before serving; if you do, the greens will become disagreeably limp.

Making and Buying Salad Dressings

A majority of the salad recipes in this book include recipes for their own custom dressings, as a creative salad often has a dressing specifically tailored to its ingredients.

But *please* do not forsake any bottled dressings you might love. I never wish to be called a snob where any food is concerned, and I would hate for you to feel that bottled dressings are unacceptable for the salads in this book.

Vinegars and Other Acidic Elements

Vinegars and other acidic ingredients contribute bracing sharpness to a salad.

BALSAMIC VINEGAR

This is the gold standard of vinegars, a speciality of Modena in Italy, made by steeping and reducing fine wine vinegar in a succession of ever-smaller wooden kegs over many years, up to several decades. It has a deep, tawny red colour and incredibly rich taste with an edge of sweetness, and the finest, oldest varieties can have an almost syrup-like consistency.

CIDER VINEGAR

Made from apple cider, this vinegar gives that fruit's characteristic tangy sweetness to dressings in which it is included.

FRUIT VINEGARS

These may be made by fermenting a fruit wine or, more commonly, by steep-

ing fresh fruit such as raspberries in wine vinegar. You'll see that, with the exception of one salad in this book, I don't specifically call for fruit vinegars; when I want a fruit-flavoured salad, I add fruit to it.

HERB VINEGARS

The same grumpy comment I made in the preceding paragraph also applies to vinegars flavoured by steeping fresh herbs in them. While some such products can be nice, and you are certainly free to substitute them for other wine-based vinegars I call for in this book, my own preference is to add fresh or dried herbs to salads or their dressings.

LEMON JUICE AND OTHER CITRUS JUICES

Sharply acidic, slightly sweet lemon juice is a fine substitute for wine vinegar in dressings intended for light salads, particularly those featuring seafood or white-meat chicken. (In a few recipes in this book, I also use orange juice to make a pleasantly sweet and tangy dressing.) Please don't resort to using bottled lemon juice; always squeeze it fresh from whole lemons. You'll note that I usually include a little sugar in the seasonings for lemon-based dressing; this not only counteracts some of its acidity but actually serves to highlight the lemony flavour in the dressing.

RICE VINEGAR

Distilled from rice wine, this light, mild vinegar works well in dressings for Asian-style salads. I prefer to buy a Japanese variety designated as 'seasoned' rice vinegar, which includes a little sugar that adds a pleasant sweet edge to dressings in which it is used.

SHERRY VINEGAR

A vinegar fermented from the fortified, cask-aged wine of Jerez in Spain, this is notable for the rich, sweet-edged, nut-like taste it shares with that wine.

WINE VINEGARS

Vinegar fermented from red or white wine and sharing all the distinctive properties of the wine from which it is made. For that reason, select good-quality wine vinegars; you may even wish to experiment with vinegars made from specific white or red wines such as Chardonnay or Pinot Noir.

Oils, Mayonnaise and Other Fats

While the acidic element of a dressing gives it and the salad much of its characteristic flavour and bracing sharpness, the oils or other fats in the dressing serve another, multiple role. First, they act as the medium by which the dressing clings, coating salad leaves and other ingredients. They also contribute richness, in taste, in body and in the way the dressing feels in the mouth. Finally, many forms of fat contribute their own distinctive flavour to a salad dressing, although some dressings instead make use of flavourless vegetable oils when a less complex flavour effect is desired. Below are some of the most common choices for oils and other salad dressing enrichments, as used in this book.

CREAM AND SOURED CREAM

Both these dairy products sometimes enrich salad dressings. Whipping cream makes a lovely dressing when combined with lemon juice, which serves to thicken it. Soured cream can add a rich note to some mayonnaise-based dressings.

MAYONNAISE

This thick emulsion of oil and egg yolks makes a wondrous enrichment for some old-fashioned salads. At one time, I used to make my own mayonnaise for salads. Today, given the widespread health concerns regarding the use of raw egg yolks, it is wiser to use commercial mayonnaise, and some excellent brands exist. When this book calls for mayonnaise, buy the best quality you can, and steer clear of products labelled 'mayonnaise dressing' or 'salad dressing' or other names that indicate it isn't pure, real mayonnaise. Note, however, that many manufacturers also now sell reduced-fat mayonnaise, which can be an excellent choice if you are trying to lower your dietary fat intake.

NUT OILS

Some specific dressing recipes may call for oils expressed from flavourful nuts, such as hazelnuts or walnuts, to contribute the rich, deep taste of that particular nut. Be sure to buy good quality products made from toasted nuts, which will have fuller flavour. You will also see groundnut or peanut oil. It has just a hint of that nut's richness, making it a good addition to Asian salads, but it is predominately flavourless and may be used as an all-purpose oil. (Note, however, that many people are severely allergic to peanuts, and that allergy extends to the oil as well.) Nut oils go rancid fairly quickly, so buy the smallest quantity you can and store in an airtight container in a cool place.

OLIVE OIL

The oil expressed from ripe olives has a rich, fruity flavour that makes it the best, most versatile oil for dressing salads. For the recipes in this book, I specify extra virgin olive oil, the designation for oil extracted on the first pressing without the use of heat or any chemical extractants.

SESAME OIL

This is an oil pressed from sesame seeds, which enriches dressings for Asian-style salads. Do not, however, buy the pale golden sesame oils sold in some health-food shops; seek, instead, Asian-style

sesame oil, which has a deep golden brown colour that results from toasting the seeds before the oil is pressed.

VEGETABLE OILS

This general term refers to oils or oil blends made from corn, rape seed or safflower seeds, noted for their light, unobtrusive flavours.

Although that sounds fairly specific, on a visit to the oils section of virtually any supermarket you'll find an incredible range of extra virgin olive oils to choose from. They vary in colour, in translucency and in taste depending on the kinds of olives they were pressed from, where they were grown, the equipment that was used and how the oil was filtered. As a rule, the darker green the colour, the stronger its flavour. Select an olive oil for salad dressings that best suits the other salad ingredients as well as your personal tastes; more specifically, whether or not you like the taste of olive oil. Note, too, that extra virgin olive oils labelled 'light' are not light on calories or fat, having just as much of both as any oil, but rather are light in flavour.

Seasonings

Most salad dressing recipes begin with stirring salt and pepper into vinegar until the salt has dissolved, with seasoning a necessary first step because the presence of oil can hamper the dissolving. Salt, as it does in most cases, heightens the flavour of the salad, with the exact amount used determined by the relative saltiness of the other ingredients. In Asian salads, soy sauce often replaces the salt. In lemon-based dressings, a little sugar joins the salt to heighten the fruity flavour. White pepper tends to replace black pepper in more delicately flavoured dishes, or in those in which you don't want black specks to mar the salad's overall appearance.

Still other seasonings go a long way to adding character to dressings. Mustard, in its creamy form, provides the extra benefit of emulsifying the dressing, giving it both body and a uniform consistency. Among the many other seasonings available, the most common are probably the various forms of fresh herbs—particularly basil, chives, dill and parsley (preferably the more flavourful flat leafed Italian variety)—that may be found in the produce sections of supermarkets.

Basic Vinaigrette

MAKES ABOUT 225ml (8fl oz)

50ml (2fl oz) wine or balsamic vinegar
½ teaspoon salt
¼ teaspoon pepper
175ml (6fl oz) extra virgin olive oil

In a small mixing bowl, stir together the vinegar, salt and pepper with a fork or small wire whisk, until the salt dissolves. Stirring continuously, slowly pour in the olive oil. Set the dressing aside until ready to use.

Variations

LEMON VINAIGRETTE

Substitute lemon juice for the vinegar, adding ½ to ¾ teaspoon sugar with the salt and pepper.

DIJON MUSTARD VINAIGRETTE

As soon as the salt and pepper have been added, stir in 1 teaspoon of Dijon mustard before adding the oil.

TEST KITCHEN NOTES

LITERALLY A 'LITTLE VINEGAR' SAUCE, THIS CLASSIC, MOST BASIC, SIMPLE AND VERSATILE SALAD DRESSING RELIES ON THE QUALITY OF THE OIL AND THE VINEGAR YOU USE. WHILE I GIVE BASIC PROPORTIONS HERE, YOU'LL FIND MANY VARIATIONS ON IT.

PROPORTIONS OF VINEGAR TO OIL CAN VARY FROM 1 PART TO 2 PARTS, 1 TO 3, OR MORE, DEPENDING AGAIN ON THE INDIVIDUAL PROPERTIES OF YOUR INGREDIENTS AND THE SALAD YOU ARE DRESSING. USE THE ACCOMPANYING RECIPE AS A STARTING POINT FOR YOUR OWN EXPERIMENTS.

Classic Blue Cheese Dressing

MAKES ABOUT 350ml (12fl oz)

115g (4oz) mayonnaise
125ml (4fl oz) soured cream
85g (3oz) blue cheese, crumbled
Black pepper

In a mixing bowl, stir together the mayonnaise, soured cream and blue cheese until evenly blended. Season to taste with black pepper, stirring it in thoroughly. Cover the bowl with cling film and refrigerate until serving time.

TEST KITCHEN NOTES

I FIND THAT BOTH MAYONNAISE AND SOURED CREAM ARE ESSENTIAL TO GET THE RIGHT BALANCE OF CREAMINESS AND RICH TANG TO BACK UP THE FLAVOUR OF THE CHEESE.

YOU MIGHT ALSO TRY CRUMBLING THE CHEESE INTO A BASIC VINAIGRETTE, ESPECIALLY ONE MADE WITH BALSAMIC VINEGAR. THE RESULTING ITALIAN-STYLE BLUE CHEESE DRESSING CAN BE SPECTACULAR ON MEATY SALADS, ESPECIALLY THOSE FEATURING STEAK.

IF YOU FRESHLY GRIND THE PEPPER, SET YOUR GRINDER TO A COARSE SETTING AND THE DRESSING WILL GIVE YOU OCCASIONAL LITTLE PUNGENT BITES OF PEPPER FLAVOUR. DON'T ADD SALT: YOU'LL GET ENOUGH FROM THE CHEESE AND MAYONNAISE.

Ranch Dressing

MAKES ABOUT 350ml (12fl oz)

175ml (6fl oz) buttermilk

175g (6oz) mayonnaise

1 teaspoon lemon juice

¼ small onion, grated

1 teaspoon finely chopped fresh chives
    or ½ teaspoon dried chives

1 teaspoon finely snipped fresh dill or
    ½ teaspoon dill weed

1 teaspoon finely chopped fresh
    flat-leaf parsley

½ –¾ teaspoon salt

In a mixing bowl, stir together the buttermilk, mayonnaise and lemon juice until smoothly blended. Add the onion and herbs and stir them in. Season to taste with salt. Cover the bowl with cling film and refrigerate until serving.

Variations

BLACK PEPPER RANCH

Add a generous spoonful of freshly ground black pepper.

CHEESE RANCH

Add some freshly grated Parmesan cheese or crumbled blue cheese.

CUCUMBER RANCH

Grate 25–55g (1–2oz) fresh cucumber and leave in a sieve for a few minutes, pressing gently to encourage excess juices to drip out. Then stir it into the dressing and adjust the seasonings to taste.

HORSERADISH RANCH

Add a little grated fresh or bottled horseradish to taste for a subtly spicy effect.

LOW-FAT RANCH

Note that most buttermilk is low in fat; to make a low-fat dressing, use reduced- or non-fat mayonnaise.

TEST KITCHEN NOTES

BASED ON BUTTERMILK AND MAYONNAISE, THIS DRESSING IS NOTED FOR ITS CREAMY CONSISTENCY AND RICH, TANGY FLAVOUR, WHICH PROVIDES A COOLING COMPLEMENT TO SPICY OR ROBUST SALADS.

Thousand Island Dressing

MAKES ABOUT 350ml (12fl oz)

225g (8oz) mayonnaise
50ml (2fl oz) tomato ketchup
55g (2oz) sweet pickled cucumber relish

In a mixing bowl, stir together the mayonnaise, ketchup and relish until thoroughly blended. Cover the bowl with cling film and refrigerate until serving time.

Russian Dressing

MAKES ABOUT 350ml (12fl oz)

125ml (4fl oz) vegetable oil
125ml (4fl oz) tomato ketchup
4 tablespoons lemon juice
2 tablespoons caster sugar
1 tablespoon Worcestershire sauce
1 teaspoon dry mustard powder
Salt
Black pepper

Put all the ingredients except the salt and pepper in a jar with a tight-fitting lid and shake vigorously until well blended. Taste the dressing; stir in salt and pepper to taste. Cover and refrigerate until serving time.

CHAPTER 3

Classics and Variations

Like legendary stars, some main meal salads are recognisable by a single name: Caesar, Cobb, Waldorf, Niçoise. They've no doubt achieved such status at least in part because of their singular power to satisfy. Nothing satiates the senses quite like a rich, garlicky Caesar; contrasts tastes and textures like a Cobb; refreshes the palate like a Waldorf; or combines lightness and heartiness quite like a Niçoise.

Another way such classics resemble true stars is their versatility—the many ways in which they can take on a wide range of different guises while retaining their inimitable identities. On the pages that follow, you'll witness this phenomenon again and again, with variations that offer refreshing updates of the reliable standards. After you've sampled a few of them, don't hesitate to try your hand at variations of your own. You might well create a new star.

Classic Caesar Salad

DRESSING

2 garlic cloves, peeled
4 anchovy fillets
3 tablespoons lemon juice
1 tablespoon Worcestershire sauce
½ teaspoon dry mustard powder
2 eggs
125ml (4fl oz) extra virgin olive oil

SALAD

2 large cos lettuces, leaves separated,
    washed and chilled
1 recipe Garlic Croûtons (see page 18)
55g (2oz) Parmesan cheese, freshly grated
16 anchovy fillets

1. First make the dressing. Bring a small saucepan of water to the boil over medium-high heat. Meanwhile, one at a time, put the garlic cloves in a garlic press and press them into a large salad bowl. Add the 4 anchovy fillets and, with the prongs of a fork, mash them together with the pressed garlic until they form a smooth paste. Stirring briskly with a small wire whisk, add the lemon juice and Worcestershire sauce. Add the mustard powder and stir until it is completely dissolved.

2. When the water is boiling, gently drop in the eggs and boil them for precisely 1 minute. Drain immediately and rinse under cold running water until the eggs are just cool enough to handle. Break the eggs carefully into the salad bowl, using a small teaspoon to scoop them out if necessary. Whisk the eggs into the other ingredients just until blended. Then, whisking continuously, pour in the olive oil in a slow, steady stream.

3. Remove the lettuce leaves from the refrigerator and reserve several of the largest outer leaves to garnish each serving. Tear the remaining leaves into bite-size pieces, dropping them into the salad bowl. Add the croûtons and sprinkle in the Parmesan cheese. If you like, add the whole anchovies; or leave them out, reserving them to garnish individual servings for those who want them. Toss the salad thoroughly with the dressing.

4. Arrange the reserved cos lettuce round the edge of large, chilled individual serving plates or bowls. Pile the salad on top. Garnish with any reserved anchovies and serve immediately.

TEST KITCHEN NOTES

WHO COULD HAVE IMAGINED THAT THE SALAD THROWN TOGETHER TO PLEASE A GROUP OF REVELLERS IN TIJUANA, MEXICO, ON THE 4TH OF JULY WEEKEND IN 1924 BY CAESAR CARDINI, AN ITALIAN-BORN CHEF, WOULD BECOME ONE OF THE WORLD'S GREATEST SALADS? THE BORDER TOWN, JUST SOUTH OF SAN DIEGO, CALIFORNIA, WAS A FASHIONABLE GETAWAY FOR STARS OF THE GROWING MOVIE INDUSTRY, WHO OVER THE COMING DECADES MADE CAESAR'S CREATION THE 'IN' SALAD AT THEIR OWN FAVOURITE WATERING HOLES.

KEEPING ITS ROOTS IN MIND, THE LIST OF DRESSING INGREDIENTS READS LIKE A BRACING HANGOVER CURE: GARLIC, ANCHOVIES, MUSTARD, WORCESTERSHIRE SAUCE AND BARELY COOKED EGGS. IF YOU'RE ANXIOUS ABOUT THE EGGS BECAUSE OF RECENT SCARES ABOUT SALMONELLA, YOU COULD INSTEAD SOFT-BOIL THEM FOR 3 TO 4 MINUTES AND USE JUST THE STILL-OOZING YOLKS. OR SUBSTITUTE 2 OR 3 TABLESPOONS OF DOUBLE CREAM, WHICH WILL GIVE A SIMILARLY RICH CONSISTENCY AND FLAVOUR.

IF YOU MUST BUY ALREADY GRATED PARMESAN, BE SURE THAT YOU CHOOSE ONE THAT IS FRESH AND NOT DRIED. AND MAKE SURE THE GRATED CHEESE YOU BUY OR PREPARE YOURSELF IS GRATED INTO FINE PARTICLES SO THAT IT BLENDS PROPERLY WITH THE OTHER CAESAR SALAD INGREDIENTS.

Light Caesar Salad with Grilled Prawns

SERVES 4

GRILLED PRAWNS

450g (1lb) raw king or tiger prawns,
    peeled and deveined
2 tablespoons lemon juice
2 tablespoons extra virgin olive oil
Salt
White pepper

DRESSING

3 garlic cloves, peeled
4 anchovy fillets, well drained
3 tablespoons lemon juice
1 tablespoon Worcestershire sauce
½ teaspoon dry mustard powder
3 tablespoons plain yogurt
125ml (4fl oz) extra virgin olive oil

SALAD

2 large cos lettuces, leaves separated,
    washed and chilled
1 recipe Fat-free Garlic Croûtons
    (see page 18)
55g (2oz) Parmesan cheese, freshly
    grated
16 anchovy fillets, well drained

1. Preheat the grill or barbecue. In a bowl, toss the prawns with the lemon juice and olive oil and leave them to marinate while you make the dressing.

2. One at a time, put the garlic cloves in a garlic press and press them into a large salad bowl. Add the 4 anchovy fillets and, with the prongs of a fork, mash them together with the pressed garlic until they form a smooth paste. Stirring briskly with a small wire whisk, add the lemon juice and Worcestershire sauce. Add the mustard powder and stir until it is completely dissolved. Whisk the yogurt into the other ingredients just until blended. Then, whisking continuously, pour in the olive oil in a slow, steady stream.

3. Remove the prawns from the marinade and discard the marinade. Season the prawns all over with salt and white pepper to taste and put them under the grill or on the barbecue, cooking them just until uniformly pink and firm, about 2 minutes per side.

4. While the prawns cook, assemble the salad. Remove the lettuce leaves from the refrigerator and reserve several of the largest outer leaves to garnish each serving. Tear the remaining leaves into bite-size pieces, dropping them into the salad bowl. Add the croûtons and sprinkle in the Parmesan. If you like, add the whole anchovies; or leave them out, reserving them to garnish individual servings for those who want them. Toss the salad thoroughly, until all the lettuce is well coated with the dressing and cheese.

5. Arrange the reserved cos lettuce leaves round the edge of large, chilled serving plates or bowls. Pile the salad on top. Garnish with any reserved anchovies and top with the grilled prawns.

TEST KITCHEN NOTES

IN AN AGE OF HEALTH-CONSCIOUS, LOW-FAT COOKING AND EATING, IT IS INEVITABLE THAT THE CAESAR SALAD WOULD COME UNDER SOME SCRUTINY, CONSIDERING ALL ITS EGGS, OLIVE OIL AND CHEESE.

THIS RECIPE REMARKABLY APPROXIMATES THE CLASSIC CAESAR, WHILE CUTTING OUT MUCH OF THE FAT. THE SECRET IS USING PLAIN LOW-FAT YOGURT TO GIVE THE DRESSING BODY AND RICHNESS. I ALSO ADD A LITTLE OLIVE OIL FOR FLAVOUR; BE SURE TO USE A GOOD EXTRA VIRGIN OIL THAT HAS A DISTINCTIVE OLIVE TASTE.

WITH ITS SPRIGHTLY FLAVOURS, THIS PARTICULAR VERSION OF THE VENERABLE CAESAR SALAD GOES VERY WELL WITH A FEW GRILLED OR BARBECUED PIECES OF SALMON AND TUNA.

Cajun Caesar Salad with Blackened Steak

SERVES 4

BLACKENED STEAK

2 tablespoons extra virgin olive oil

4 teaspoons Cajun-style blackened spice
    blend or to taste

4 fillet steaks, about 175g (6oz) each,
    well trimmed of fat

DRESSING

4 garlic cloves, peeled

4 anchovy fillets, well drained

3 tablespoons lemon juice

1 tablespoon Worcestershire sauce

1 teaspoon Tabasco sauce

½ teaspoon dry mustard powder

2 eggs

125ml (4fl oz) extra virgin olive oil

SALAD

2 large cos lettuces, leaves separated,
    washed and chilled

1 recipe Garlic-Spice Croûtons
    (see page 18)

55g (2oz) Parmesan cheese, freshly
    grated

1. Preheat the grill or barbecue. In a bowl, use a fork to stir together the olive oil and Cajun spices to form a paste. Add the steaks, turning them in the paste and smearing them evenly with it. Leave them to marinate at room temperature while you make the dressing.

2. Bring a small saucepan of water to the boil over medium-high heat. Meanwhile, one at a time, put the garlic cloves in a garlic press and press them into a large salad bowl. Add the 4 anchovy fillets and, with the prongs of a fork, mash them together with the garlic until they form a smooth paste. Stirring briskly with a small wire whisk, add the lemon juice, Worcestershire sauce and Tabasco sauce. Add the mustard powder and stir until dissolved.

3. When the water is boiling, gently drop in the eggs and boil them for precisely 1 minute. Drain immediately and rinse under cold running water until the eggs are just cool enough to handle. Break the eggs carefully into the salad bowl, using a small teaspoon to scoop them out if necessary. Whisk the eggs into the other ingredients just until blended. Then, whisking continuously, pour in the olive oil in a slow, steady stream.

4. Put the steaks coated with their spice paste under the grill or on the barbecue. Cook them to your liking, about 4 minutes per side for medium-rare.

5. While the steaks cook, assemble the salad. Remove the lettuce leaves from the refrigerator, reserving several large outer leaves as garnish. Tear the remaining leaves into bite-size pieces, dropping them into the salad bowl. Add the croûtons and sprinkle in the Parmesan. Toss the salad thoroughly, until well coated with the dressing and cheese.

6. Arrange the reserved whole leaves on large, chilled individual serving plates. Pile the salad on top. Cut each steak crossways into 1cm (½in) thick slices and arrange them atop the salads, drizzling any juices from the cutting board over the meat. Serve immediately.

TEST KITCHEN NOTES

THE CLASSIC CAESAR HAS ALWAYS HAD AN UNSPOKEN REPUTATION AS A ROBUST SALAD. THIS RECIPE IS PEPPED UP BY ADDING MORE GARLIC AND A SHAKE OF TABASCO SAUCE IN THE DRESSING AND TOPPING IT WITH WELL-SEASONED STEAK.

Caesar Salad with Chilli Chicken Breast

SERVES 4

CHIPOTLE CHICKEN BREAST

1 x 200g (7oz) can chipotle chillies in sauce

4 boneless, skinless chicken breasts, 115–175g (4–6oz) each

Salt

Black pepper

DRESSING

3 garlic cloves, peeled

4 anchovy fillets, well drained

3 tablespoons lemon juice

1 tablespoon Worcestershire sauce

½ teaspoon dry mustard powder

2 eggs

125ml (4fl oz) extra virgin olive oil

SALAD

2 large cos lettuces, leaves separated, washed and chilled

1 x 280g (10oz) bag tortilla chips

55g (2oz) Parmesan cheese, freshly grated

1. Preheat the grill or barbecue. In a bowl, use a fork to mash together the chipotles with their sauce until they form a coarse paste. Add the chicken breasts, coating them evenly with the paste. Leave them to marinate at room temperature while you make the dressing.

2. Bring a small saucepan of water to the boil over medium-high heat. Meanwhile, one at a time, put the garlic cloves in a garlic press and press them into a large salad bowl. Add the 4 anchovy fillets and, with the prongs of a fork, mash them together with the garlic to form a smooth paste. Stirring briskly with a small wire whisk, add the lemon juice and Worcestershire sauce. Add the mustard powder and stir until dissolved.

3. Gently drop the eggs in the boiling water and boil precisely 1 minute. Drain immediately and rinse under cold running water until the eggs are just cool enough to handle. Break the eggs into the salad bowl, using a teaspoon to scoop them out if necessary. Whisk the eggs into the other ingredients just until blended. Then, whisking continuously, pour in the olive oil in a slow, steady stream.

4. Remove the chicken breasts from their chipotle marinade and, depending on how intensely spiced you want them, wipe off some or most of the paste, discarding it. Season the chicken breasts all over to taste with salt and pepper and put them under the grill or on the barbecue. Cook them just until evenly done, about 5 minutes per side.

5. While the chicken breasts cook, assemble the salad. Remove the lettuce leaves from the refrigerator. Discard any tough, large outer leaves and tear the remaining leaves into bite-size pieces, dropping them into the salad bowl. Add three-quarters of the tortilla chips, breaking them coarsely into bite-size pieces; sprinkle in the Parmesan. Toss the salad thoroughly with the dressing.

6. Pile the salad on top of large, chilled individual serving plates or bowls. Arrange the remaining chips round each salad. Cut each chicken breast crossways into 1cm (½in) thick slices and arrange them on top of the salads. Serve immediately.

TEST KITCHEN NOTES

THE STRONG FLAVOURS OF CAESAR SALAD STAND UP VERY WELL TO THE SMOKY INTENSITY OF THE CHILLI-MARINATED CHICKEN.

AFTER HANDLING CHILLIES, TAKE CARE TO WASH YOUR HANDS THOROUGHLY WITH WARM SOAPY WATER AND AVOID TOUCHING YOUR EYES OR ANY CUTS OR OTHER SENSITIVE AREAS.

Roast Beef and Bitter Greens Cobb with Balsamic-Blue Cheese Vinaigrette

SERVES 4

DRESSING

6 tablespoons balsamic vinegar
115g (4oz) blue cheese, crumbled
¼ teaspoon salt
2 teaspoons dried oregano
175ml (6fl oz) extra virgin olive oil

SALAD

4 eggs
350g (12oz) smoked streaky bacon, thinly
    sliced
900g (2lb) mixed rocket, radicchio,
    chicory, frisée or cos lettuce
4 plum tomatoes
2 ripe avocados, preferably Hass variety
2 tablespoons lemon juice
450g (1lb) cold roast beef, cut into 1cm
    (½in) chunks

1. First make the dressing. In a mixing bowl, use a fork to stir together the balsamic vinegar, blue cheese and salt until the salt dissolves completely and the cheese slightly. With your fingertips, crumble in the oregano and stir briefly to combine. Stirring briskly, slowly pour in the olive oil until fully incorporated. Set the dressing aside.

2. Put the eggs in a saucepan of cold water and bring to the boil over medium-high heat. As soon as the water starts to boil, check the time and cook the eggs for 10 minutes. Drain well, rinse with cold running water and set the eggs aside.

3. While the eggs are boiling, cook the bacon. Arrange the rashers side by side in one or two frying pans and cook over medium heat, turning frequently, until crisp and brown, about 10 minutes. Remove the bacon and set aside to drain on several layers of kitchen paper towel.

4. With your fingers, tear large salad leaves into small, bite-size pieces. Arrange the leaves in an even bed in a large salad bowl or large individual serving bowls.

5. Cut out and discard the tough cores of the tomatoes. Cut them in half and, with a finger, poke out the seeds. Coarsely chop the tomatoes and arrange in a neat section on top of the salad.

6. Halve, stone and peel the avocados. Cut them into bite-size chunks, put them in a small bowl and gently toss with the lemon juice to coat. Arrange the avocado in a neat section on top of the leaves.

7. Peel the eggs and coarsely chop them. Arrange the eggs in another section on top of the leaves.

8. Crumble or chop the bacon into small, bite-size pieces and arrange them on top of the leaves.

9. Finally, arrange the beef chunks on top of the leaves.

10. Serve the large salad or individual portions at the table, passing the dressing separately. Alternatively, dress and toss the salad in the kitchen before serving.

TEST KITCHEN NOTES

THINK OF THIS AS A HEARTY SALAD, WITH MORE ROBUST-TASTING BITTER GREENS FORMING THE BACKDROP FOR THE MEAT. I'VE TAKEN THE LIBERTY OF ADDING THE BLUE CHEESE TO THE DRESSING. FOR AN ESPECIALLY RICH EFFECT, SUBSTITUTE GORGONZOLA CHEESE.

Classic Cobb Salad

SERVES 4

DRESSING

4 tablespoons lemon juice
½ teaspoon salt
½ teaspoon white pepper
½ teaspoon caster sugar
2 tablespoons Dijon mustard
175ml (6fl oz) extra virgin olive oil

SALAD

4 eggs
350g (12oz) smoked streaky bacon, thinly
   sliced
2 large cos lettuces, leaves separated,
   washed and chilled
4 large plum tomatoes
2 ripe avocados, preferably Hass variety
2 tablespoons lemon juice
450g (1lb) cooked turkey breast, cut into
   1cm (½in) chunks
225g (8oz) blue cheese, crumbled

1. First make the dressing. In a mixing bowl, use a fork or small wire whisk to stir together the lemon juice, salt, pepper and sugar until the salt and sugar dissolve. Stir in the mustard until smooth. Stirring briskly, slowly pour in the olive oil until fully incorporated. Set the dressing aside.

2. Put the eggs in a saucepan of cold water and bring to the boil over medium-high heat. As soon as the water starts to boil, check the time and cook the eggs for 10 minutes. Drain well, rinse with cold running water and set the eggs aside.

3. While the eggs are boiling, cook the bacon. Arrange the rashers side by side in one or two frying pans and cook over medium heat, turning frequently, until crisp and brown, about 10 minutes. Remove the bacon and set aside to drain on several layers of kitchen paper towel.

4. Remove the lettuce leaves from the refrigerator, discarding any large, tough outer leaves. With your fingers or with a sharp knife, break or cut the lettuce into small, bite-size pieces. Arrange the lettuce in an even bed in a large salad bowl or large individual serving bowls.

5. Cut out and discard the tough cores of the tomatoes. Cut them in half and, with a finger, poke out the seeds. Coarsely chop the tomatoes and arrange in a neat section on top of the salad.

6. Halve, stone and peel the avocados. Cut them into bite-size chunks, put them in a small bowl and gently toss with the lemon juice to coat. Arrange the avocado in a neat section on top of the lettuce.

7. Shell the eggs and cut them into wedges. Arrange the eggs in another section on top of the lettuce.

8. Crumble or chop the bacon into small, bite-size pieces and arrange them on top of the lettuce.

9. Finally, arrange the turkey pieces and the blue cheese on top of the lettuce.

10. Serve the large salad or individual portions at the table, passing the dressing separately. Alternatively, dress and toss the salad in the kitchen before serving.

TEST KITCHEN NOTES

BOB COBB OF HOLLYWOOD'S LEGENDARY BROWN DERBY RESTAURANT CAME UP WITH THIS NOW-CLASSIC AMERICAN SALAD BACK IN 1936. ITS APPEAL LIES, I THINK, IN THE WEALTH OF SENSORY EXPERIENCES IT OFFERS IN A SINGLE BOWL.

WHEN PRESENTING A COBB SALAD, MANY PEOPLE ENJOY THE BEAUTIFUL CONTRASTS OF COLOUR AND SHAPE THAT COME FROM THE VARIOUS INGREDIENTS ON TOP OF THE BED OF LETTUCE. BUT THAT LEAVES YOU HAVING TO TOSS THE ENTIRE SALAD OR INDIVIDUAL SERVINGS AT THE TABLE, A MESSY PROSPECT. I RECOMMEND TOSSING THE SALAD IN THE KITCHEN BEFORE SERVING.

Thai Cobb Salad with Chicken and Ginger-Mint Dressing

SERVES 4

DRESSING

6 tablespoons seasoned rice vinegar

1½ tablespoons finely chopped
fresh root ginger

1 tablespoon soy sauce

2 teaspoons caster sugar

1 tablespoon finely chopped fresh
mint leaves

125ml (4fl oz) vegetable oil

SALAD

4 eggs

900g (2lb) mixed salad greens

4 plum tomatoes

225g (8oz) cooked chicken meat, cut into
1cm (½in) chunks

225g (8oz) char siu (Chinese barbecued
pork), diced

225g (8oz) mozzarella or fontina cheese,
cut into 1cm (½in) cubes

4 small pickled gherkins, cut into 1cm
(½in) chunks

55g (2oz) dry-roasted peanuts

4 sprigs fresh mint, for garnish

1. First make the dressing. In a mixing bowl, use a fork or small wire whisk to stir together the rice vinegar, ginger, soy sauce and sugar until the sugar dissolves. Stir in the mint. Stirring briskly, slowly pour in the vegetable oil until fully incorporated. Set the dressing aside.

2. Put the eggs in a saucepan of cold water and bring to the boil over medium-high heat. As soon as the water starts to boil, check the time and cook the eggs for 10 minutes. Drain well, rinse with cold running water and set the eggs aside.

3. Arrange the salad greens in an even bed in a large salad bowl or large individual serving bowls.

4. Cut out and discard the tough cores of the tomatoes. Cut each in half and, with a finger, poke out the seeds. Coarsely chop the tomatoes and arrange in a neat section on top of the salad.

5. Peel the eggs and coarsely chop them. Arrange the eggs in another section on top of the salad.

6. Arrange the chicken, char siu, cheese and gherkins on top of the salad. Scatter the peanuts on top. Garnish with mint sprigs.

7. Serve the large salad or individual portions at the table, passing the dressing separately. Alternatively, dress and toss the salad in the kitchen before serving.

TEST KITCHEN NOTES

THIS SALAD IS BASED ON TRADITIONAL SOUTH-EAST ASIAN DISHES. WHAT ALL THESE DISHES HAVE IN COMMON IS A DRESSING THAT PULLS THE SALAD TOGETHER IN AN EYE-OPENING WAY.

IN PLACE OF THE BACON TRADITIONALLY USED IN COBB SALADS, I CALL HERE FOR CHAR SIU, CHINESE-STYLE BARBECUED PORK. YOU'LL FIND THIS LEAN, SWEETLY SPICED COOKED PORK IN CHINESE DELIS, OR YOU MIGHT BE ABLE TO GET A PORTION 'TO TAKE AWAY' FROM A CHINESE RESTAURANT. ALTERNATIVELY, USE THICKLY SLICED HONEY-CURED COOKED HAM.

Greek Prawn and Spinach Cobb Salad

SERVES 4

DRESSING

Lemon Vinaigrette (see page 25)

SALAD

4 eggs
225g (8oz) smoked streaky bacon, thinly
    sliced
900g (2lb) young spinach leaves,
    thoroughly washed and patted dry
2 red peppers, quartered and seeded
2 ripe avocados, preferably Haas variety
2 tablespoons lemon juice
450g (1lb) cooked peeled prawns
225g (8oz) feta cheese, crumbled
25g (1oz) pine nuts, toasted (see page
    17)

1. Prepare the dressing and set aside.

2. Put the eggs in a saucepan of cold water and bring to the boil over medium-high heat. As soon as the water starts to boil, check the time and cook the eggs for 10 minutes. Drain well, rinse with cold running water and set the eggs aside.

3. While the eggs are boiling, cook the bacon. Arrange the rashers side by side in one or two frying pans and cook over medium heat, turning frequently, until crisp and brown, about 10 minutes. Remove the bacon and set aside to drain on several layers of kitchen paper towel.

4. Arrange the spinach in an even bed in a large salad bowl or large individual serving bowls.

5. Cut the pepper quarters in half lengthways. Then cut them crossways into strips about 5mm (¼ in) thick. Arrange the peppers in sections on top of the spinach.

6. Halve, stone and peel the avocados. Cut them into bite-size chunks, put them in a small bowl and gently toss with the lemon juice to coat. Arrange the avocado in a neat section on top of the spinach.

7. Peel the eggs and coarsely chop them. Arrange the eggs in another section on top of the spinach.

8. Crumble or chop the bacon into small, bite-size pieces and arrange them on top of the spinach.

9. Finally, arrange the prawns and the feta cheese on top of the spinach. Garnish with pine nuts.

10. Serve the large salad or individual portions at the table, passing the dressing separately. Alternatively, dress and toss this delicious salad in the kitchen before serving.

TEST KITCHEN NOTES

ALTHOUGH THIS VARIATION MIGHT LOOK AND TASTE DIFFERENT FROM THE CLASSIC COBB, IT DOES FOLLOW THE BASIC FORMULA.

BABY SPINACH LEAVES REPLACE THE COS LETTUCE. YOU COULD SUBSTITUTE ROUND LETTUCE LEAVES, OR STICK WITH THE CLASSIC COS. COOKED PRAWNS TAKE THE PLACE OF THE TURKEY OR CHICKEN. THAT'S A SIMPLE SWAP OF ONE PROTEIN FOR ANOTHER. YOU COULD ALSO TRY COOKED CRABMEAT. STANDING IN FOR THE TOMATO ARE STRIPS OF RED PEPPER, WHICH ALSO REPLACE SOME OF THE CRISPNESS LACKING IN THE SPINACH. YOU COULD, HOWEVER, STAY WITH TOMATO IF YOU PREFER. AND FETA CHEESE ASSUMES THE ROLE OF THE BLUE CHEESE.

Classic Waldorf Salad with Poached Chicken

SERVES 4

450ml (16fl oz) chicken stock

450g (1lb) boneless, skinless chicken breasts

4 apples

4 tablespoons lemon juice

4 sticks celery, cut into 1cm (½in) wide pieces

115g (4oz) shelled walnut halves or pieces, toasted (see page 17)

2–3 tablespoons finely snipped fresh chives

325g (11oz) mayonnaise

225g (8oz) radicchio or round lettuce leaves

1. In a medium-size saucepan, bring the stock to the boil over medium-high heat. Add the chicken breasts, reduce the heat to low and simmer gently, covered, until the chicken is cooked through, about 10 minutes. Leave the chicken to cool to room temperature in the stock. Reserve the stock, if you wish, and transfer the chicken to a bowl, cover and refrigerate until cold.

2. Quarter and core the apples and cut them into 1cm (½in) chunks. Immediately put them in a large mixing bowl and toss with the lemon juice to coat them well to prevent them from discolouring.

3. Cut or tear the chicken into 1cm (½in) chunks and add them to the bowl. Add the celery pieces.

4. Reserve several of the most attractive walnut halves or pieces to garnish the salad. Add the remainder to the bowl along with the chives and the mayonnaise. Toss well to mix and coat the ingredients. If you plan to serve the salad later, cover with cling film and refrigerate.

5. Arrange the radicchio or round lettuce leaves to form a bed on large, chilled individual serving plates or shallow bowls. Mound the salad mixture in the centre and garnish with the reserved nuts.

TEST KITCHEN NOTES

OSCAR TSCHIRKY, MAÎTRE D'HÔTEL OF THE WALDORF-ASTORIA HOTEL IN NEW YORK, DEVELOPED THIS SALAD IN THE LATE 1890S. THE NOW-STANDARD WALNUTS THAT MOST PEOPLE FIND SO PLEASING WERE A LATER ADDITION, FIRST APPEARING IN PRINT AROUND 1928.

WITH ITS SWEETNESS, CRISPNESS AND THE MILD RICHNESS OF A MAYONNAISE DRESSING, THE WALDORF RAPIDLY FOUND FAVOUR AS A LIGHT LUNCHEON SPECIALITY. I ADMIT TO HAV- ING TAKEN THE VERY SLIGHT LIBERTY HERE OF ADDING THE SORT OF POACHED CHICKEN THAT NO DOUBT OFTEN ACCOMPANIED THIS SALAD ON EARLY MENUS.

FOR EFFECT, CHOOSE A RED-SKINNED, FAIRLY CRISP EATING APPLE SUCH AS A ROYAL GALA OR SPARTAN. YOU COULD ALSO, IF YOU WISH, USE A MIXTURE OF RED APPLES AND GREEN OR YELLOW VARIETIES SUCH AS GOLDEN DELICIOUS, GRANNY SMITH OR JONAGOLD.

Waldorf Salad with Pears, Prosciutto, Gruyère, Hazelnuts and Orange Mayonnaise

SERVES 4

6 large pears

125ml (4fl oz) orange juice

4 sticks celery, cut into 1cm (½in) wide pieces

115g (4oz) hazelnuts, toasted (see page 17) and skins rubbed off

115g (4oz) Parma ham, cut into thin strips

2 tablespoons finely chopped fresh mint leaves

225g (8oz) mayonnaise

225g (8oz) mixed baby salad greens

1 head chicory, leaves separated

Fresh mint sprigs, for garnish

1. Quarter and core the pears. Cut 4 of them into 1cm (½in) chunks and the remainder into slender lengthways wedges. Immediately put all the pear pieces in a large mixing bowl and toss gently with the orange juice to coat them well to prevent them from discolouring. Remove the wedges and set them aside.

2. Add the celery to the pear chunks together with the hazelnuts, Parma ham and chopped mint. Add the mayonnaise and toss well to mix and coat the ingredients. If you plan to serve the salad later, cover with cling film and refrigerate.

3. Arrange the mixed greens to form a bed on large, chilled individual serving plates or shallow bowls. Mound the salad mixture in the centre and arrange the pear wedges and chicory leaves round it. Garnish with mint sprigs.

TEST KITCHEN NOTES

THE CONCEPT FOR THIS SALAD REMAINS CLOSE TO OSCAR TSCHIRKY'S ORIGINAL. PEARS REPLACE THE APPLES, HAZELNUTS THE WALNUTS. THIN STRIPS OF *PROSCIUTTO DI PARMA*, THE FAMOUS, VELVETY DRIED RAW HAM OF PARMA, ITALY, GO BEAUTIFULLY WITH PEARS. (IF YOUR BUDGET DOESN'T ALLOW FOR IT, SUBSTITUTE SOME STRIPS OF ANY GOOD COOKED HAM.) AND GRUYÈRE CHEESE—OR EMMENTHAL OR ANY GOOD SWISS—IS ADDED FOR THE SAME REASON.

USE ANY VARIETY OF PEAR THAT IS AVAILABLE, BUT TRY TO SELECT THOSE THAT, THOUGH RIPE, ARE FAIRLY FIRM SO THAT THEY WILL HOLD THEIR SHAPE IN THE SALAD.

Summer Fruit Waldorf Salad with Pecans and Prawns

SERVES 4

900g (2lb) peaches
450g (1lb) plums
450g (1lb) cherries
4 sticks celery, cut into 1cm (½in) wide
    pieces
4 tablespoons lemon juice
1 tablespoon finely grated lemon zest
115g (4oz) shelled pecan halves or
    pieces, toasted (see page 17)
450g (1lb) cooked prawns
225g (8oz) mayonnaise
450g (1lb) round lettuce leaves
Fresh mint sprigs, for garnish

1. With a sharp knife, halve the peaches and plums, remove their stones and cut the fruit into 1–2.5cm (½–1in) chunks. Set aside a few attractive pieces for garnishing and put the remainder into a large mixing bowl.

2. Reserve several attractive whole cherries with stalks for garnishing. With a small, sharp knife, halve the remainder and remove their stones. Put the cherry halves in the bowl with the other fruit.

3. Add the celery to the bowl together with the lemon juice and zest. Toss well to coat all the ingredients.

4. Set aside a few attractive pecan halves or pieces and put the remainder into the bowl. Add the prawns and the mayonnaise and toss well to mix and coat the ingredients. If you plan to serve the salad later, cover with cling film and refrigerate.

5. Arrange the lettuce leaves to form a bed on large, chilled individual serving plates or shallow bowls. Mound the salad mixture in the centre and garnish with the reserved fruit pieces, nuts and mint sprigs.

TEST KITCHEN NOTES

WHAT A REFRESHING SURPRISE THIS WALDORF SALAD VARIATION IS, ESPECIALLY IF YOU, AS I DO, LOVE SUMMER FRUIT. IF YOU TAKE CARE TO SELECT FRUIT THAT IS ABSOLUTELY RIPE YET STILL FIRM ENOUGH TO BE CUT UP AND HOLD ITS SHAPE, THE SALAD WILL HAVE A JEWEL-LIKE BEAUTY AND EVERY BITE WILL BE FILLED WITH SWEET JUICE.

USE THE ACCOMPANYING INGREDIENT QUANTITIES ONLY AS A STARTING POINT FOR YOUR OWN VARIATIONS. IF YOU ESPECIALLY LIKE CHERRIES, USE MORE. INCLUDE SOME NECTARINES IN PLACE OF THE PEACHES, IF YOU WISH. I FIND THE TARTNESS OF SOME PLUMS' SKIN A BRACING CONTRAST TO THE OTHER FLAVOURS; BUT IF THEY DISTRACT YOU, PEEL THE PLUMS, OR LEAVE THEM OUT ENTIRELY.

Classic Salade Niçoise

SERVES 4

DRESSING

2 tablespoons white wine vinegar

1 teaspoon lemon juice

¼ teaspoon salt

¼ teaspoon caster sugar

1 tablespoon Dijon mustard

6 tablespoons extra virgin olive oil

SALAD

350g (12oz) potatoes

4 eggs

225 (8oz) thin green beans, trimmed and
    cut into pieces about 4cm (1½in)
    long

2 tablespoons capers, drained

4 plum tomatoes, cut into thin wedges

115g (4oz) black olives, halved and pit-
    ted

2 x 200g (7oz) cans tuna in oil, drained

1 x 55g (2oz) can anchovy fillets in oil,
    drained (optional)

1 tablespoon finely chopped fresh chives

1 tablespoon finely chopped parsley

2 round lettuces, leaves separated

1. First make the dressing. In a small bowl, use a fork or small wire whisk to stir together the vinegar, lemon juice, salt and sugar until the salt and sugar dissolve. Stir in the mustard until blended. Stirring briskly, pour in the oil in a thin, steady stream. Set aside.

2. Put the potatoes in a saucepan with lightly salted cold water to cover. Bring to the boil over medium-high heat and cook until tender when pierced with the tip of a small, sharp knife, 15 to 20 minutes.

At the same time, put the eggs in another saucepan of cold water and bring to the boil over medium-high heat. As soon as the water starts to boil, check the time and cook the eggs for 10 minutes. Drain well, rinse with cold running water and set the eggs aside.

Drain and peel the potatoes while still hot. Let them cool, then cut into 1cm (½in) cubes and place in a mixing bowl.

3. Meanwhile, bring yet another saucepan of salted water to the boil over medium-high heat. Add the green beans and cook until tender but still crisp, 3 to 4 minutes. Drain and rinse under cold running water until cool. Drain well and add to the potatoes.

4. Add the capers, tomatoes, olives, tuna and, if using, the anchovies to the mixing bowl. Scatter with the chives and parsley.

Pour the dressing over the salad ingredients and toss gently but well until evenly coated.

5. Arrange the lettuce leaves on individual serving plates to form attractive beds. Spoon the salad mixture on to the beds of lettuce.

TEST KITCHEN NOTES

SOME PEOPLE LIKE TO ARRANGE THE FEATURED INGREDIENTS NEATLY ON TOP OF THE BED OF LETTUCE. I FEEL, HOWEVER, THAT *SALADE NIÇOISE* HAS A COMFORTABLE INFORMALITY THAT CALLS FOR IT TO BE TOSSED, AS HERE, AND I RESERVE THE MORE STYLISED PRESENTATIONS FOR THE FRESH FISH VARIATIONS THAT FOLLOW.

Salade Niçoise with Seared Fresh Tuna, Fresh Mozzarella and Beefsteak Tomato

SERVES 4

DRESSING

4 tablespoons caster lemon juice

2 teaspoons sugar

1½ tablespoons Dijon mustard

175ml (6fl oz) extra virgin olive oil

SALAD

4 fillets fresh tuna, about 115g (4oz) each

2 tablespoons extra virgin olive oil

2 tablespoons lemon juice

4 eggs

175g (6oz) rocket

2 beefsteak tomatoes, about 280g (10oz) each

450g (1lb) mozzarella cheese, preferably buffalo mozzarella

Salt

Black pepper

1 tablespoon capers, drained

115g (4oz) black olives, drained

4 tablespoons finely shredded fresh basil leaves

1. First make the dressing. In a small bowl, use a fork or small wire whisk to stir together the lemon juice and sugar until the sugar dissolves. Stir in the mustard until blended. Stirring briskly, pour in the oil in a thin, steady stream until fully incorporated. Set aside.

2. Put the tuna fillets in a shallow bowl large enough to hold them in a single layer. Add the olive oil and lemon juice, turn the fillets to coat them and leave at room temperature to marinate.

3. Preheat the grill or barbecue.

4. Put the eggs in a saucepan of cold water and bring to the boil over medium-high heat. As soon as the water starts to boil, check the time and cook the eggs for 10 minutes. Drain well, rinse with cold running water and set the eggs aside.

5. Toss the rocket leaves with a few spoonsful of the dressing and arrange them in a bed on one side of four serving plates.

6. With a small, sharp knife, cut out the cores of the tomatoes. Cut the tomatoes in half through their stalk ends, then cut them crossways into 5mm (¼in) thick slices. Cut the mozzarella into slices of the same thickness. Arrange the tomato and cheese slices overlapping across the other half of each plate and spoon some more of the dressing over them.

7. Shell the hard-boiled eggs, cut them into quarters and arrange them on each plate.

8. Season the tuna fillets with salt and black pepper and cook them under the grill or on the barbecue just until nicely seared, about 2 minutes per side. Cut each fillet crossways into slices about 1cm (½in) thick and array them on top of the beds of rocket.

9. Spoon more dressing liberally over the tomatoes and mozzarella and on top of the tuna. Garnish with the capers, olives and fresh basil and serve immediately.

TEST KITCHEN NOTES

THE COOKING INSTRUCTIONS GIVEN PRODUCE TUNA THAT IS SEARED—THAT IS, COOKED ROUND THE EDGES AND STILL ROSY PINK IN THE MIDDLE. YOU MAY, IF YOU WISH, COOK IT LONGER THAN INSTRUCTED, BUT TAKE CARE NOT TO OVERCOOK TO THE POINT OF DRYNESS.

Salade Niçoise with Poached Salmon

SERVES 4

DRESSING

4 tablespoons lemon juice

2 teaspoons caster sugar

1½ tablespoons finely snipped fresh dill

175ml (6fl oz) extra virgin olive oil

SALAD

450ml (16fl oz) dry white wine

450g (1lb) centre-cut salmon fillet, cut
    crossways into 4 equal portions

Salt

White pepper

350g (12oz) new potatoes

2 eggs

225g (8oz) sugar snap peas, trimmed
    and stringed (see notes)

350g (12oz) round lettuce leaves

8 large leaves chicory

2 plum tomatoes

8 pickled whole beetroots

115g (4oz) black olives, drained

Fresh dill sprigs, for garnish

1. First make the dressing. In a small bowl, use a fork or small wire whisk to stir together the lemon juice and sugar until the sugar dissolves. Stir in the dill. Stirring briskly, pour in the oil in a thin, steady stream. Set aside.

2. Pour the wine into a non-reactive saucepan just big enough to hold the salmon fillets side by side. Bring the wine to the boil over medium-high heat; then reduce the heat to very low. Season the salmon fillets all over with salt and white pepper to taste and carefully place them in the pan. Cover and poach the salmon until the fillets are firm and completely opaque, checking by gently separating the flakes of one with the tip of a small, sharp knife. With a spatula, gently lift the fillets from the liquid and transfer them to a plate. Let them cool briefly, then cover with cling film and refrigerate.

3. Put the potatoes in a saucepan with lightly salted cold water to cover. Bring to the boil over medium-high heat and cook until tender when pierced with the tip of a small, sharp knife, 10 to 15 minutes.

At the same time, put the eggs in another saucepan of cold water and bring to the boil over medium-high heat.

TEST KITCHEN NOTES

FRESH SALMON POACHED IN WHITE WINE AND THEN ALLOWED TO COOL MAKES A LOVELY VARIATION ON THE CLASSIC TUNA. FOR THE BEST FLAVOUR AND FEWEST BONES, ASK YOUR FISHMONGER TO CUT THE FILLETS FROM THE CENTRE OF A SIDE OF SALMON.

SMALL, FRESH SUGAR SNAP PEAS CAN BE EATEN RAW, BUT ARE GENERALLY AT THEIR BEST IF BRIEFLY PARBOILED, FOLLOWING THE RECIPE INSTRUCTIONS. BEFORE COOKING, TRIM AND STRING THE BEANS: WITH YOUR INDEX FINGER AND THUMB, SNAP THE STALK END OF EACH POD AND PULL ALONG THE STRAIGHT SEAM OF THE POD TO REMOVE THE FIBROUS STRINGS.

AN ALTERNATIVE TO SUGAR SNAP PEAS WOULD BE THE MORE COMMONLY AVAILABLE MANGETOUT. OR YOU COULD USE SLENDER SPEARS OF ASPARAGUS.

THE SALMON, POTATOES, EGGS AND SUGAR SNAPS CAN BE COOKED SEVERAL HOURS AHEAD OR THE NIGHT BEFORE AND REFRIGERATED.

As soon as the water starts to boil, check the time and cook the eggs for 10 minutes. Drain well, rinse with cold running water and set the eggs aside.

Drain the potatoes. If the skins look unattractive, peel them off while the potatoes are still warm; otherwise, leave them on. Let the potatoes cool, then cut each one into 4 wedges. Put them in a small bowl and toss gently with just enough of the dressing to coat them. Set aside.

4. Meanwhile, bring yet another saucepan of salted water to the boil over medium-high heat. Add the sugar snap peas and parboil for 1 minute. Immediately drain them and rinse under cold running water until cool. Drain well and set aside.

5. Arrange the lettuce leaves in a bed on chilled individual serving plates. Place a salmon fillet across the centre of each plate. Mound some of the potato salad next to the salmon fillet.

6. Peel the eggs and cut each lengthways into quarters. Nestling a wedge of egg near each chicory leaf, place 2 leaves and 2 wedges on each plate.

7. With a small, sharp knife, cut out the cores of the tomatoes. Cut the tomatoes lengthways in quarters and arrange the tomato wedges on each plate.

8. Cut the beetroots into quarters. Arrange the peas and the beetroots on each plate.

9. Spoon more dressing liberally over the salmon, sugar snap peas, egg wedges, tomatoes and beetroot. Garnish with the olives and fresh dill sprigs and serve immediately.

CHAPTER 4

Chopped Salads

After much deliberation, I think I've finally figured out why chopped salads have become so popular: they remind us of nursery food, chopped up into easy-to-eat pieces that, with every bite, whisk us back to happy childhood meals. Consider that the next time you see powerful business people ordering them for lunch.

Whether featuring cured meats or seafood, chopped salads seem to be the most popular of the genre. That doesn't mean, however, that the concept can't extend far and wide to other ingredients, as the recipes in this chapter demonstrate.

Whichever salads you plan to make, I recommend that you make a small investment in a large wooden chopping bowl and a *mezzaluna*, the Italian-style half-moon-shaped chopper. Working with these two basic tools, you can put a chopped salad together in next to no time and the work is extremely satisfying. Alternatively, you could pre-chop all the ingredients to the required size with a knife on a cutting board before tossing them with the dressing in a large salad bowl. The work will take a little bit longer, however, and you're not likely to have nearly as much fun.

Farmer's Style Vegetarian Chopped Salad

SERVES 4

DRESSING

4 tablespoons red wine vinegar
½ teaspoon salt
¼ teaspoon white pepper
175ml (6fl oz) extra virgin olive oil

SALAD

2 carrots, cut into 1cm (½in) thick slices
2 green peppers, quartered and seeded
2 sticks celery, cut into 1cm (½in) thick
   slices
1 cucumber, peeled, halved lengthways
   and seeded
8 radishes, trimmed and thickly sliced
1 small red onion, coarsely chopped
2 tablespoons finely chopped fresh flat-
   leaf parsley
2 tablespoons finely shredded fresh basil
   leaves
400g (14oz) ricotta cheese, drained
25g (1oz) Parmesan cheese, freshly
   grated
1 round lettuce, leaves separated
Crostini (see page 19)
Fresh flat-leaf parsley sprigs, for garnish

1. In a small mixing bowl, stir together the vinegar, salt and pepper until the salt dissolves. Stirring continuously with a fork or small whisk, pour in the olive oil in a thin, steady stream, beating until emulsified. Set aside.

2. Put the carrots, peppers, celery, cucumber, radishes and red onion in a large wooden chopping bowl. With a mezzaluna, chop into coarse pieces. Add the parsley, basil, ricotta and Parmesan. Continue gently chopping and tossing the mixture until finely chopped into pieces about 5mm (¼in) across. Still tossing the mixture, add the dressing, thoroughly blending the salad.

3. Arrange the lettuce leaves to form beds on large, chilled individual serving plates. Mound the salad in the centre of each plate. Garnish with Crostini and parsley sprigs.

Crostini (see page 19)

TEST KITCHEN NOTES

My mother and grandmother used to make a version of this chopped salad for themselves on hot summer days. You can change the vegetables around to suit your own taste, but make sure that the ones you do include are really crisp.

Some red pepper would be a colourful substitute for the green. Jícama, a Mexican root vegetable with a crisp apple-like flesh, would be an especially nice embellishment. A little raw fennel bulb would add a refreshing hint of anise flavour. You could also include some spring onions along with the red onion. For more subtle notes, supplement the herbs with other fresh ones like chives, dill or chervil.

Neptune Chopped Salad

SERVES 4

DRESSING

Thousand Island Dressing (see page 27)

SALAD

1 iceberg lettuce, cored and
    quartered
1 cos lettuce, tough outer leaves
    discarded, remaining leaves
    separated and chilled
2 red peppers, quartered and seeded
1 cooked lobster tail, about 225g (8oz),
    shelled and meat cut into 1cm (½in)
    thick slices
225g (8oz) cooked crabmeat, picked
    over to remove any gristle or shell
225g (8oz) cooked prawns
1 ripe but firm avocado, preferably
    Hass variety
2 tablespoons finely chopped fresh
    basil leaves
2 tablespoons finely chopped
    fresh chives
225g (8oz) frisée, coarsely torn
Lemon-Garlic Croûtons (see page 18)

1. Prepare the dressing and set
it aside.

2. Put the iceberg and cos lettuce in a
large wooden chopping bowl. With a
mezzaluna, begin chopping them in the
bowl until coarsely chopped. Add the
peppers, lobster, crabmeat and prawns.

3. Quarter, stone and peel the avocado
and add it to the bowl. Continue chopping and tossing the mixture until it is
chopped into pieces about 1cm (½in)
across. Add the basil and chives. While
tossing the mixture with the mezzaluna,
add just enough of the dressing to coat
the salad well.

4. Arrange the leaves round the edge
of individual plates. Spoon the salad into
the centre of the plates and garnish with
the Lemon-Garlic Croûtons.

TEST KITCHEN NOTES

HERE I'VE ADDED A FEW MORE INGREDIENTS TO THIS CLASSIC SALAD TO BRING IT UP TO DATE. COS, MIXED WITH THE ICEBERG IN EQUAL PARTS, CONTRIBUTES A SLIGHTLY MORE ROBUST LETTUCE FLAVOUR. RED PEPPER ADDS BRIGHT COLOUR, CRISPNESS AND A SWEETNESS TO COMPLEMENT THAT OF THE SEAFOOD. AVOCADO ALSO COM-PLEMENTS THEM WITH ITS RICH TASTE AND TEX-TURE. FRESH HERBS ADD STILL MORE SPARK. AND THE CROÛTONS BRING A MUCH-NEEDED CRUNCH.

IF YOU CAN'T GET THE THREE TYPES OF SHELLFISH CALLED FOR, JUST BUY EXTRA QUAN-TITIES OF THOSE THAT ARE AVAILABLE; DON'T LET THE SHORTAGE OF A LOBSTER TAIL, FOR EXAMPLE, DEPRIVE YOU OF A DELICIOUS CHOPPED SALAD EXPERIENCE.

Traditional Italian Chopped Salad with Red Kidney Beans and Soppressata

SERVES 4

DRESSING

4 tablespoons balsamic vinegar

½ teaspoon salt

¼ teaspoon black pepper

175ml (6fl oz) extra virgin olive oil

SALAD

2 large cos lettuces, tough outer leaves discarded, remaining leaves separated

175g (6oz) soppressata or other Italian-style salami

175g (6oz) provolone cheese, sliced

1 x 425g (15oz) can red kidney beans, rinsed and drained

2 red peppers, roasted, peeled and seeded (see pages 15–16), then torn into long strips, juices reserved

2 tablespoons finely chopped fresh chives

2 tablespoons finely chopped fresh flat-leaf parsley

2 tablespoons toasted pine nuts (see page 17)

12 black olives

1. First make the dressing. In a small mixing bowl, stir together the balsamic vinegar, salt and black pepper until the salt dissolves. Stirring continuously with a fork or small whisk, pour in the olive oil in a thin, steady stream, beating until emulsified. Set aside.

2. Put the cos lettuce leaves in a large wooden chopping bowl. With a mezza-luna, begin chopping them in the bowl until coarsely chopped. Add the soppressata, provolone, kidney beans, roasted peppers, chives and parsley and continue chopping and tossing the mixture until finely chopped into pieces about 5mm (¼in) across. Still tossing the mixture, add the dressing and the toasted pine nuts.

3. Spoon the salad into individual shallow pasta serving bowls. Garnish with olives.

TEST KITCHEN NOTES

SOPPRESSATA IS A HIGHLY FLAVOURFUL TYPE OF ITALIAN PORK SALAMI. YOU COULD SUBSTITUTE ANOTHER ITALIAN SALAMI OR PARMA HAM. WHICHEVER TYPE OF CURED MEAT YOU USE, MAKE SURE TO BUY IT THINLY SLICED, WHICH WILL HELP YOU CHOP IT UP.

THE SAME SLICING INSTRUCTIONS APPLY TO THE PROVOLONE CHEESE. YOU COULD ALSO SUBSTITUTE MOZZARELLA (PREFERABLY FRESH), THOUGH IT DOESN'T SLICE AS NEATLY.

IF YOU'RE PRESSED FOR TIME, BUY A JAR OF ROASTED RED PEPPERS. PACKED IN OIL OR VINEGAR, USUALLY WITH SUGAR AND SPICES, THEY'LL MAKE A VERY TASTY SUBSTITUTE FOR THE HOME-ROASTED PEPPERS CALLED FOR.

Tuna and White Bean Chopped Salad

SERVES 4

DRESSING

4 tablespoons fresh lemon juice

1 teaspoon caster sugar

½ teaspoon salt

¼ teaspoon white pepper

175ml (6fl oz) extra virgin olive oil

SALAD

2 large heads radicchio, leaves separated

2 large cos lettuces, tough outer leaves discarded, remaining leaves separated and chilled

1 red pepper, quartered and seeded

2 x 200g (7oz) cans tuna in olive oil, drained

2 x 425g (15oz) cannellini beans, rinsed well and drained

2 tablespoons finely chopped fresh chives

2 tablespoons finely snipped fresh dill

2 tablespoons finely chopped fresh flat-leaf parsley

2 large shallots, coarsely chopped

4 small sprigs fresh chervil, dill or flat-leaf parsley, for garnish

1. In a small mixing bowl, stir together the lemon juice, sugar, salt and white pepper until the sugar and salt dissolve. Stirring continuously with a fork or small whisk, pour in the olive oil in a thin, steady stream, beating until emulsified. Set aside.

2. Cut the radicchio leaves into long strips and evenly distribute among four individual serving plates.

3. Put the cos lettuce leaves and red pepper quarters in a large wooden chopping bowl. With a mezzaluna, begin chopping them in the bowl until coarsely chopped. Add the tuna, cannellini beans, chives, dill and parsley and continue chopping and tossing the mixture until finely chopped into pieces about 5mm (¼in) across. Add the shallots. While tossing the mixture, add just enough of the dressing to coat the salad well.

4. Spoon the salad on to the beds of radicchio leaves. Garnish with chervil, dill or parsley sprigs.

TEST KITCHEN NOTES

TONNO E FAGIOLI, A TRADITIONAL ITALIAN APPETISER OF CANNED TUNA TOSSED WITH CANNELLINI (WHITE KIDNEY) BEANS, WAS THE INSPIRATION FOR THIS CHOPPED SALAD. FOR THE MOST AUTHENTIC TASTE, I RECOMMEND THAT YOU USE TUNA PACKED IN OLIVE OIL, ALTHOUGH YOU COULD, IF YOU WISH, MAKE IT WITH BRINE-PACKED TUNA AND STILL GET GOOD RESULTS.

JUST A HINT OF PARMA HAM—SAY, 55–85G (2–3OZ) FOR FOUR SALADS—ADDS A SUBTLE EDGE OF SALTY RICHNESS TO THE SALAD, A NICE COMPLEMENT TO THE TUNA. ANOTHER OPTION WOULD BE TO INCLUDE A FEW ANCHOVY FILLETS.

LARGE OUTER LEAVES FROM A GOOD-SIZED RADICCHIO MAKE A NICELY CONTRASTING BED ON WHICH TO PRESENT THE SALAD. IF YOU CAN'T FIND RADICCHIO, USE ANY LETTUCES THAT COME TO HAND—PERHAPS THE OUTER LEAVES YOU'D OTHERWISE DISCARD FROM THE COS LETTUCE.

Spring Chicken Chopped Salad with Herbed Lemon Cream Dressing

SERVES 4

CHICKEN AND SPRING VEGETABLES

1 litre (1¾ pints) chicken stock

2 medium carrots, cut crossways into 1cm (½in) thick slices

24 asparagus spears, trimmed

450g (1lb) boneless, skinless chicken breasts

DRESSING

4 tablespoons lemon juice

¾ teaspoon caster sugar

¾ teaspoon salt

¼ teaspoon white pepper

225ml (8fl oz) double cream, chilled

2 tablespoons finely chopped fresh basil

2 tablespoons finely chopped fresh chives

2 tablespoons finely snipped fresh dill

SALAD

2 red peppers, quartered and seeded

2 shallots, coarsely chopped

1 cucumber, peeled, halved lengthways and seeded

350g (12oz) mixed baby salad leaves

1. First prepare the chicken and vegetables. In a wide saucepan, bring the stock to the boil over medium-high heat. Add the carrots and asparagus and simmer until crisp but still tender, about 3 minutes. Remove the vegetables with a slotted spoon and set aside in a bowl to cool, then cover and chill in the refrigerator.

2. Put the chicken in the simmering stock, cover and cook, turning the chicken occasionally, until it is cooked through, 7 to 10 minutes. Remove the chicken from the stock with a slotted spoon and leave to cool, then cover and chill in the refrigerator.

3. Before assembling the salad, make the dressing. In a mixing bowl, use a wire whisk to stir together the lemon juice, sugar, salt and pepper until the salt dissolves. Whisking continuously, slowly pour in the cream, continuing to whisk until the mixture is thick but still fluid. Stir in the herbs.

4. With a sharp knife, cut off the tips of the asparagus spears and reserve them. In a large wooden chopping bowl, combine the remaining asparagus stalks with the carrots, peppers, shallots and cucumber. With your fingers, tear the cooked chicken into chunks and add them to the bowl.

Using a mezzaluna, chop the ingredients, turning and tossing the mixture until you have pieces about 5mm–1cm (¼–½in) across. Pour in enough of the dressing to coat the pieces evenly to your liking, using the mezzaluna to toss the mixture.

5. Arrange beds of mixed baby greens on individual plates and mound the chopped salad on top. Garnish with the asparagus tips.

TEST KITCHEN NOTES

IF ONE CHOPPED SALAD ALONE HAS THE POWER TO SUMMON THE ESSENCE OF SPRINGTIME, THIS IS IT—TENDER-CRISP VEGETABLES, A BOUQUET OF FRESH HERBS AND CHUNKS OF POACHED CHICKEN BREAST, ALL ENVELOPED IN A CREAMY, TANGY DRESSING.

YOU COULD MAKE THE SALAD, IF YOU WISH, WITH LEFT-OVER CHICKEN, WHITE MEAT OR DARK, FROM THE PREVIOUS EVENING'S ROAST. I FIND, HOWEVER, THAT IT TASTES ALL THE BETTER AND MORE SUCCULENT WHEN YOU FRESHLY POACH THE CHICKEN BREASTS AN HOUR OR TWO BEFORE SERVING TIME.

Chopped Chef's Salad

DRESSING

Classic Blue Cheese or Ranch Dressing
(see pages 25 and 26)

SALAD

2 iceberg lettuces, 12 outer leaves
reserved, remainder cored and
quartered

1 small red onion, quartered

115g (4oz) roast turkey breast, thinly
sliced

115g (4oz) roast beef, thinly sliced

115g (4oz) cooked ham, thinly sliced

115g (4oz) mature Cheddar cheese,
thinly sliced

115g (4oz) Gruyère cheese, thinly sliced

2 tablespoons finely chopped fresh flat-
leaf parsley

4 plum tomatoes, cored and cut into thin
wedges

1. Prepare the dressing and set it aside.

2. Put the iceberg lettuce wedges and red onion quarters in a large wooden chopping bowl. With a mezzaluna, begin chopping them in the bowl until coarsely chopped. Add the turkey, beef, ham, Cheddar and Gruyère cheeses and parsley and continue chopping and tossing the mixture until finely chopped into pieces about 5mm (¼in) across. Still tossing with the mezzaluna, add enough of the dressing to coat the salad well.

3. Arrange the reserved iceberg leaves to form bowl shapes on individual serving plates. Mound the salad in the centre. Garnish with tomato wedges.

TEST KITCHEN NOTES

I HAVE LONG FOUND THE CLASSIC CHEF'S SALAD TO BE DISCONCERTING IN ITS PRESENTATION. WITH ALL THE FEATURED INGREDIENTS CUT INTO BIG STRIPS AND LAID OUT IN NEAT SECTIONS ON TOP OF THE LETTUCE, I WOULD BE REDUCED TO COMPOSING INDIVIDUAL BITES ON MY FORK BY FIRST SPEARING A SINGLE STRIP OF TURKEY, THEN BEEF, THEN HAM, SUPPLEMENTING THEM WITH A LITTLE CHEESE AND THEN FINALLY SPEARING A CHUNK OF LETTUCE. NEXT CAME THE STRUGGLE TO GET THE WHOLE THING INTO MY MOUTH. THE SOLUTION TO THIS DILEMMA, OF COURSE, WAS TO CHOP ALL THE INGREDIENTS TOGETHER.

HERE, I'VE ADDED JUST A HINT OF SWEET RED ONION, A MUCH BETTER WAY TO ENJOY ITS FLAVOUR THAN THE UNWIELDY RINGS OF ONION SOME CHEFS USE AS A GARNISH. YOU COULD JUST AS WELL CHOP INTO THE SALAD SOME RAW OR ROASTED PEPPER.

I'VE ALWAYS PREFERRED MY CHEF'S SALADS WITH A CREAMY DRESSING LIKE BLUE CHEESE OR RANCH, WHICH I CALL FOR HERE. OF COURSE, YOU COULD DRESS THE SALAD WITH A VINAIGRETTE, OR USE YOUR FAVOURITE BRAND OF BOTTLED THOUSAND ISLAND OR OTHER DRESSING.

Deli-Style Chopped Chef's Salad

SERVES 4

DRESSING

Russian Dressing (see page 27)

SALAD

1 medium red cabbage, cored, 6 outer
    leaves reserved, remainder quar-
    tered and cut crossways into thin
    slices
1 medium iceberg lettuce, 6 outer leaves
    reserved, remainder cored and
    quartered
1 sweet mild onion, quartered
2 large pickled gherkins, drained well
    and cut lengthways into spears
225g (8oz) salt beef, thinly sliced
225g (8oz) pastrami, thinly sliced
225g (8oz) Gruyère cheese, thinly sliced
2 medium carrots, grated
2 tablespoons finely chopped fresh flat-
    leaf parsley
4 plum tomatoes, cored and cut into thin
    wedges
Toasted bagel chips (optional)

1. Prepare the dressing and set
it aside.

2. Bring a kettle of water to the boil.
Separate the red cabbage into shreds and
arrange them in a metal sieve or colander. Pour the boiling water from the kettle evenly over the shreds to wilt them
all. Rinse with cold running water and
drain.

3. Put the cabbage, iceberg lettuce
wedges, onion quarters and gherkins in
a large wooden chopping bowl. With a
mezzaluna, coarsely chop. Add the salt
beef, pastrami and Gruyère cheese and
continue chopping and tossing the mixture until finely chopped into pieces
about 5mm (¼in) across. Add the carrots
and parsley. Still tossing with the mezzaluna, add enough of the dressing to coat
the salad well.

4. Arrange the reserved red cabbage
and iceberg leaves to form bowl shapes
on individual serving plates. Mound the
salad in the centre. Garnish with tomato
wedges and toasted bagel chips, if using.

Chilli Beef Chopped Taco Salad

SERVES 4

DRESSING

Ranch Dressing (see page 26)

SALAD

2 tablespoons olive oil
1 onion, finely chopped
1 tablespoon chilli powder or to taste
450g (1lb) extra lean minced beef
2 medium iceberg lettuces, cored and
    cut into quarters
2 x 425g (15oz) cans kidney beans,
    rinsed and drained
2 ripe but firm avocados
175g (6oz) Cheddar cheese, thinly sliced
2 tablespoons finely chopped fresh
    coriander leaves
225g (8oz) tortilla or corn chips
125ml (4fl oz) fresh tomato salsa
Fresh coriander sprigs, for garnish

1. First make the dressing and set it aside.

2. In a heavy frying pan, heat the olive oil over medium heat. Add the onion and sauté, stirring frequently with a wooden spoon, for about 1 minute. Sprinkle in the chilli powder and sauté, stirring continuously, until it is fragrant, about 30 seconds more. Add the minced beef and continue sautéing, stirring frequently to break up the meat into coarse chunks, until it is evenly browned, about 5 minutes more. Set the beef aside.

3. Put the iceberg lettuce wedges in a large wooden chopping bowl. With a mezzaluna, begin chopping them in the bowl until coarsely chopped. Add the cooked beef and kidney beans.

4. Quarter, stone and peel the avocados and add them to the bowl along with the cheese and coriander. Continue chopping and tossing the mixture until finely chopped into pieces about 5mm (¼in) across.

5. With your hands, coarsely crush in about three-quarters of the tortilla or corn chips, reserving the rest for a garnish. Still tossing with the mezzaluna, add the dressing to coat the salad well.

6. Mound the salad on to large, chilled individual serving plates or bowls. Arrange the remaining chips round the edge of the salad. Spoon large dollops of the salsa on top of each salad and garnish with coriander sprigs.

Scandinavian Chopped Herring Salad with Beetroot, Potato, Apple, Onion and Gherkin

SERVES 4

DRESSING

4 tablespoons cider vinegar

½ teaspoon caster sugar

¼ teaspoon salt

¼ teaspoon white pepper

175ml (6fl oz) vegetable oil

SALAD

2 medium boiling potatoes

2 green apples

1 small red onion, quartered

12 small sweet pickled gherkins, drained well

12 small pickled beetroots, drained

2 x 175g (6oz) jars pickled herring fillets in wine, drained

2 tablespoons coarsely snipped fresh dill

1 round lettuce

Fresh dill sprigs, for garnish

1. In a small mixing bowl, stir together the vinegar, sugar, salt and pepper until the sugar and salt dissolve. Stirring continuously with a fork or small whisk, pour in the vegetable oil in a thin, steady stream. Set aside.

2. Put the potatoes in a small saucepan of water and bring to the boil over medium-high heat. Boil until the potatoes are tender when pierced with the tip of a small, sharp knife, 15 to 20 minutes. Drain well. While still hot, carefully peel the potatoes and cut them into quarters. Set aside.

3. Quarter and core the apples and put them in a large wooden chopping bowl with the red onion and gherkins. With a mezzaluna, begin chopping them in the bowl until coarsely chopped. Add the potatoes, beetroots, herring pieces and dill and continue gently chopping and tossing the mixture until finely chopped into pieces about 5mm (¼in) across. Still tossing the mixture with the mezzaluna, add the dressing to coat the salad well. Transfer to a non-reactive glass or ceramic bowl, cover and chill in the refrigerator for at least 1 hour.

4. Arrange the lettuce leaves on individual serving plates. Mound the salad in the centre of each plate. Garnish with dill sprigs.

TEST KITCHEN NOTES

PICKLED HERRING IS A REFINED TASTE, BUT NOTHING ELSE OFFERS QUITE THE SAME COMBINATION OF FLAVOUR, BRACING TANG AND SATISFYING MEATINESS.

HERRING ON ITS OWN CAN BE PRETTY POWERFUL, TO BE TAKEN IN MEASURED DOSES. THAT IS WHY I LIKE THIS SCANDINAVIAN-INSPIRED SALAD SO MUCH, PARTNERING THE HERRING AS IT DOES WITH SEVERAL COMPLEMENTARY INGREDIENTS—POTATOES, APPLES, ONION, GHERKINS AND PICKLED BEETROOTS.

OFFER THIS DELICIOUS, PUNGENT SALAD AS A SPECIAL LUNCH FOR HERRING-LOVING FRIENDS. SERVE WITH A LOAF OF GOOD, FRESHLY BAKED BLACK BREAD OR RYE BREAD, CUT INTO ULTRA-THIN SLICES IN THE SCANDINAVIAN STYLE; SOME SOFTENED, UNSALTED BUTTER; AND VERY WELL CHILLED BEER OR ICED AQUAVIT—BOTH OF WHICH HAVE THE ABILITY TO CLEANSE AND REFRESH THE PALATE AFTER EVERY SINGLE BITE.

Chopped Tropical Fruit Salad with Coconut Cream Dressing

SERVES 4

1 ripe pineapple

1 ripe mango

1 ripe paw paw

4 navel oranges

175g (6oz) jicama, peeled and
    cut into 1cm (½in) thick slices

2 tablespoons lime juice

115g (4oz) shelled macadamia nuts,
    toasted (see page 17)

225ml (8fl oz) canned coconut cream

2 tablespoons finely chopped fresh
    mint leaves

12 whole cos lettuce leaves

1 ripe kiwi fruit, peeled and cut into
    5mm (¼in) thick slices

Fresh mint sprigs, for garnish

1. With a large, sharp knife, cut off the top and bottom of the pineapple. Stand the pineapple upright and, slicing downwards, peel away its skin in thick strips. With the tip of a small, sharp knife, cut out any remaining tough 'eyes' from the fruit. With the pineapple still upright, cut downwards to slice the fruit away from the thick, woody central core; discard the core.

2. With a small, sharp knife, peel the mango. Then, cut the fruit away from the large, flat central stone in thick slices. Set aside with the pineapple.

3. Halve, peel and seed the paw paw and cut it lengthways into 1cm (½in) thick slices. Set them aside with the mango and pineapple.

4. With a sharp knife, cut off the ends of the oranges in slices thick enough to reveal the fruit. One at a time, stand the oranges on their navel ends and cut off the peel in strips thick enough to remove the membranes and reveal the fruit. Holding each orange in your hand over a mixing bowl, use a small, sharp knife to cut between the fruit and membrane of each segment, allowing it to drop into the bowl.

5. Put the jícama slices in a large wooden chopping bowl. With a mezzaluna, chop them into pieces about 2.5cm (1in) across. Add the lime juice and toss gently to coat the jícama.

6. Add the pineapple, mango, paw paw and orange segments and continue chopping until you have pieces about 1cm (½in) in size.

Add the macadamia nuts, coconut cream and chopped mint leaves and, with the mezzaluna, gently fold the mixture together. Transfer to a bowl, cover and chill in the refrigerator for at least 1 hour.

7. Arrange the cos lettuce leaves on individual serving plates. Mound the salad in the centre and garnish with kiwi slices and mint sprigs.

TEST KITCHEN NOTES

HERE IS AN EXOTIC TWIST ON A CLASSIC FRUIT SALAD, MADE ALL THE MORE ACCESSIBLE BY THE EVER-INCREASING AVAILABILITY OF GOOD TROPICAL FRUIT. THE SMALL PIECES OF JICAMA, A REFRESHINGLY CRISP ROOT VEGETABLE FROM MEXICO, ADD A SURPRISING, PLEASANT CONTRAST TO THE COMBINATION OF RICHLY PERFUMED, SWEET FRUITS.

WORTH SEEKING OUT ARE PACKETS OF WHOLE FRESH PINEAPPLES THAT HAVE ALREADY BEEN PEELED AND CORED AND ARE READY FOR YOU TO CUT UP AS THE RECIPE REQUIRES.

CHAPTER 5

Robust Salads

This chapter is about salads abounding with grilled steak, fried chicken or sizzling sausage; salads that dazzle the taste buds with exotic spices or such intense flavours as sharp, creamy goat's cheese, mustardy fruits or hot and spicy peanut dressing; salads that offer the comfort of *al dente* pasta or boiled potatoes—salads, in short, that satisfy.

The concept of robust salads might at first seem to fly in the face of convention. In general, one expects a salad to be light. But all the abovementioned suggestions offer convincing solutions to the conundrum. Through judicious measures of meaty or other rich elements, through seasonings that satiate the senses and through favourite ingredients guaranteed to fill you up, a salad can be robust even as it also retains its characteristic lightness, leaving you feeling pleasantly refreshed, as a good salad should.

Buffalo Chicken Salad

DRESSING

225ml (8fl oz) Ranch Dressing (see
   page 26)

SALAD

4 boneless, skinless chicken breasts,
   115–175g (4–6oz) each

175ml (6fl oz) spicy barbecue sauce

1 large red onion, cut into 1cm (½in)
   thick slices

25g (1oz) unsalted butter, melted

Salt

Black pepper

2 cos lettuces, leaves torn into bite-size
   pieces

4 sticks celery, cut crossways into
   5mm (¼in) slices

24 pitted black olives, cut in half

Garlic Toasts (see page 19)

2 tablespoons finely chopped fresh flat-
   leaf parsley

1. Make the dressing and set aside.

2. Preheat the grill or barbecue.

3. Meanwhile, put the chicken breasts
in a bowl and pour 125ml (4fl oz) of the
barbecue sauce over them; reserve the
remaining sauce for serving. Turn the

chicken well to coat evenly and leave to
marinate for about 15 minutes.

4. Brush the onion slices with the
melted butter and season well with salt
and pepper. Leaving the chicken breasts
thickly coated with the sauce, season
with salt and pepper and arrange them
and the onion slices on the grill or barbecue rack. Cook until the chicken and
onions are cooked through and well
browned, about 5 minutes per side.

5. While the chicken and onions are
cooking, prepare the salad. Put the
lettuce in a large mixing bowl and toss
well with the dressing. Arrange the
lettuce in beds on large, chilled individual serving plates.

6. When the chicken and onions are
done, separate the onions into rings and
strew them on top of the lettuce. Cut
each chicken breast crossways into slices
5mm–1cm (¼–½in) wide and arrange
the slices on each salad. Drizzle the
remaining barbecue sauce over the
chicken. Scatter the celery and black
olives on top and tuck the Garlic Toasts
around the side of each salad. Garnish
with parsley and serve immediately.

TEST KITCHEN NOTES

BUFFALO-STYLE CHICKEN WINGS—SERVED IN A SPICY COATING AND ACCOMPANIED BY CELERY STICKS AND A BLUE CHEESE DIP—HAVE A DEFINITE APPEAL: THE CONTRAST OF TENDER CHICKEN MEAT AND THE CRISP CELERY; THE HOT TANG OF THE CHICKEN'S SAUCE PLAYING OFF THE COOL CREAMINESS OF THE DIP; AND THE DIVINE MESSINESS OF THE WHOLE CONCEPT.

THOSE TEMPTING ASPECTS OF THE POPU-LAR APPETISER INSPIRED THIS SALAD. THE WINGS ARE REPLACED BY BONELESS, SKINLESS CHICKEN BREASTS, WHICH ARE FAR EASIER TO EAT IN A SALAD AND MUCH HEALTHIER AS WELL. THE CELERY IS THINLY SLICED AND USED AS A CRUNCHY TOPPING. A BED OF CRISP COS LET-TUCE SEEMED TO ME TO BE THE PERFECT BASE FOR THE WHOLE CONSTRUCTION. TO ROUND THINGS OFF, I'VE ALSO ADDED GRILLED RED ONION, WHICH GOES SO WELL WITH BARBE-CUED CHICKEN, A FEW PITTED BLACK OLIVES AND SOME CRISP GARLIC TOASTS. THE COMBINED EFFECT OF THESE INGREDIENTS IS OUTRAGEOUSLY SATISFYING.

BBLT Salad

SERVES 4

DRESSING

225ml (8fl oz) Ranch Dressing (see page 26)
1½ tablespoons bottled grated horseradish

SALAD

225g (8oz) smoked streaky bacon, thinly sliced
2 cos lettuces, leaves separated and torn into bite-size pieces
350g (12oz) roast beef, thinly sliced
24 cherry tomatoes, cut in half
2 tablespoons coarsely chopped fresh flat-leaf parsley

1. To make the dressing, put the Ranch Dressing in a mixing bowl and stir in the horseradish. Set aside.

2. Before assembling the salad, cook the bacon. Arrange the rashers side by side in one or two frying pans and cook over medium heat, turning frequently, until crisp and brown, about 10 minutes. Remove the bacon and set aside to drain on several layers of kitchen paper towel.

3. To assemble the salad, arrange the lettuce on large individual serving plates. Drape the slices of roast beef evenly on top of the lettuce. Arrange the cherry tomatoes on top of the beef. Crumble or chop the bacon, scatter over the salads and garnish with parsley. Serve the dressing separately or drizzle it over each salad.

TEST KITCHEN NOTES

HOW TO TRANSLATE THE APPEAL OF A BACON, LETTUCE AND TOMATO SANDWICH INTO A SALAD—THAT'S THE CHALLENGE I POSED TO MYSELF WHEN STARTING TO DEVELOP THIS RECIPE. BUT SOMETHING WAS NEEDED TO TRANSFORM THIS FAVOURITE INTO A TRULY ROBUST SALAD.

THAT MISSING INGREDIENT, FOR ME, WAS ROAST BEEF (THE EXTRA 'B' OF THE TITLE), WHICH GOES SO WELL WITH ALL THE OTHER ELEMENTS. THE SOURCE FOR THE BEEF COULD BE LAST NIGHT'S ROAST OR YOU COULD BUY IT SLICED TO ORDER FROM THE DELICATESSEN.

CHERRY TOMATOES, I FOUND, LOOK VERY PRETTY ON THE SALAD. YOU COULD SUBSTITUTE ORDINARY TOMATOES OR GO ONE BETTER AND INCLUDE SOME GOLDEN CHERRY OR BABY PLUM TOMATOES.

THE FINISHING TOUCH COMES WITH ADDING A LITTLE GRATED HORSERADISH TO A TRADITIONAL RANCH DRESSING. THERE'S NOT ENOUGH OF THE FIERY ROOT HERE TO MAKE YOUR EYES WATER, THOUGH; I'VE INCLUDED JUST ENOUGH TO MAKE YOU STOP AND TAKE NOTICE OF THE INTERESTING TASTE IT CONTRIBUTES.

ACCOMPANY THE SALAD WITH SOME SORT OF TOASTED BREAD, SUCH AS PARMESAN TOASTS (SEE PAGE 19) OR JUST CHUNKS OF A HOT CRUSTY LOAF.

Potato Salad with Grilled Sausage and Whole-Grain Mustard Dressing

SERVES 4

DRESSING

3 tablespoons cider vinegar
½ teaspoon caster sugar
¼ teaspoon salt
¼ teaspoon white pepper
1 heaped tablespoon whole-grain
    German-style or grainy
    Dijon mustard
2 tablespoons finely chopped
    fresh chives
125ml (4fl oz) vegetable oil

SALAD

900g (2lb) waxy yellow potatoes
4 German-style weisswurst or bratwurst,
    115–175g (4–6oz) each
175g (6oz) small spinach leaves,
    thoroughly washed, stalks removed
    and coarsely torn
175g (6oz) radicchio leaves, coarsely torn
12 whole chives, for garnish

1. Preheat the grill.

2. First, make the dressing. In a bowl large enough to hold the potatoes, use a fork or small wire whisk to stir together the vinegar, sugar, salt and white pepper until the sugar and salt dissolve. Add the mustard and stir until blended. Stir in the chives. Stirring continuously, pour in the oil in a thin, steady stream.

3. Put the potatoes in a large saucepan with lightly salted cold water to cover. Bring to the boil over medium-high heat; boil until tender enough to be pierced with the tip of a small, sharp knife, 15 to 20 minutes.

4. At the same time you start the potatoes, puncture each weisswurst in several places with a fork and put them in a saucepan with cold water to cover. Bring to the boil over medium-high heat. As soon as the water reaches a full rolling boil, drain well.

5. As soon as the potatoes are done, drain them well. One at a time, hold the hot potatoes in a folded tea towel to protect your hand and, with a small, sharp knife, cut them into slices about 1cm (½in) thick, letting the slices fall into the bowl of dressing. Use wooden spoons to toss the potatoes gently and let them stand at room temperature until tepid.

6. Put the drained sausages on the grill rack and grill them until evenly browned, 3 to 4 minutes per side.

7. While the sausages grill, toss together the spinach and radicchio and arrange the leaves on large individual serving plates. Mound the potato salad on top of the bed of leaves.

8. When the sausages are done, cut each one crossways on the diagonal into slices about 1cm (½in) thick. Arrange the slices on top of the potatoes, garnish with chives and serve immediately.

> **TEST KITCHEN NOTES**
>
> POTATO SALAD—WARM POTATOES TOSSED WITH A DRESSING WHICH THEY SOAK UP AS THEY COOL—IS A PERFECT ACCOMPANIMENT TO GRILLED FRESH SAUSAGES. I'VE TAKEN THE LIBERTY OF SLICING THE SAUSAGE AND OF ADDING THE MUSTARD THAT IS USUALLY DABBED ON EACH BITE OF SAUSAGE TO THE POTATO SALAD DRESSING.

Indonesian Chicken Salad with Hot and Spicy Peanut Dressing

SERVES 4

DRESSING

1½ tablespoons vegetable oil

2–4 fresh red or green chillies, according
  to taste

2.5cm (1in) piece fresh root ginger

1 medium shallot

1 teaspoon anchovy paste or *nam pla*
  (fish sauce)

225g (8oz) chunky peanut butter

175ml (6fl oz) water

125ml (4fl oz) canned coconut milk

2 tablespoons honey

1½ tablespoons seasoned rice vinegar

1½ tablespoons soy sauce

SALAD

400ml (14fl oz) chicken stock

1 tablespoon soy sauce

4 thin slices fresh root ginger

225g (8oz) mangetout, trimmed

225g (8oz) bean sprouts

2 medium carrots, thinly sliced

350g (12oz) skinless chicken breasts

1 head Chinese leaf

2 red peppers, halved, seeded and cut
  lengthways into thin strips

55g (2oz) prawn crackers

2 tablespoons finely chopped fresh
  coriander

1. Prepare the vegetables and chicken at least 2 hours and up to 24 hours before serving time. Put the chicken stock, soy sauce and ginger slices in a medium saucepan and bring to the boil over medium-high heat. Add the mangetout and parboil until just tender, about 2 minutes, removing them with a slotted spoon and transferring them to a bowl. Do the same with the bean sprouts, cooking them for about 30 seconds; then the carrot slices, cooking them for about 2 minutes.

2. Reduce the heat under the pan of stock to very low, add the chicken, cover and poach until cooked through, about 15 minutes. Leave the chicken to cool in the stock for about 30 minutes. Transfer the chicken and stock to the bowl with the vegetables, cover with cling film and refrigerate until cold.

3. To assemble the salads, cut the head of Chinese leaf crossways into 5mm (¼in) wide strips, discarding the core. On large individual serving plates, arrange the cabbage, mangetout, bean sprouts and carrots in attractive beds. Cut the chicken crossways into

5mm–1cm (¼–½in) pieces and arrange them on top with slices of red pepper.

4. To make the dressing, put the oil in a medium saucepan. With the fine side of a grater, grate the chillies, ginger and shallot directly into the pan and add the anchovy paste. Put the pan over medium-low heat and stir the mixture with a wooden spoon to combine the ingredients into a smooth paste. As soon as the paste begins to sizzle, add the peanut butter, water, coconut milk, honey, rice vinegar and soy sauce. Continue stirring the mixture until it is heated through, adding a little more water if necessary to give it a thick but fluid consistency.

5. Spoon the hot dressing generously over each salad. Garnish the salads with prawn crackers and coriander and serve immediately.

TEST KITCHEN NOTES

THIS IS A VERSION OF *GADO GADO*, INDONESIA'S TRADITIONAL AND SPECTACULAR VEGETABLE SALAD, IN WHICH ALL MANNER OF COLD, RAW OR PARBOILED VEGETABLES ARE TOSSED WITH A SIMMERED, SPICED DRESSING BASED ON PEANUT BUTTER. TRADITIONAL RECIPES CALL FOR THE ADDITION OF *NAM PLA*, A PUNGENT-SMELLING SAUCE MADE FROM FERMENTED FISH. YOU CAN USED ANCHOVY PASTE INSTEAD.

Chinese Streetmarket Chicken Chow Mein Salad

SERVES 4

SALAD

400ml (14fl oz) chicken stock

1 tablespoon soy sauce

4 thin slices fresh root ginger

350g (12oz) boneless, skinless chicken meat

225g (8oz) dried Chinese thin egg noodles

225g (8oz) bean sprouts

4 spring onions, thinly sliced

1 cucumber, coarsely grated

1 large carrot, coarsely grated

3 tablespoons finely chopped fresh coriander

225g (8oz) spinach leaves, thoroughly washed

Fresh coriander sprigs, for garnish

DRESSING

175g (6oz) sesame paste (*tahini*)

3 tablespoons seasoned rice vinegar

1 tablespoon soy sauce

1 tablespoon finely grated fresh root ginger

1 tablespoon caster sugar

4–6 tablespoons hot water

1. If making the chicken fresh for this salad, prepare it at least 2 hours and up to 24 hours before serving time. Put the chicken stock, soy sauce and ginger slices in a medium saucepan and bring to the boil over medium-high heat. Reduce the heat to very low, add the chicken, cover and poach until cooked through, 10 to 15 minutes. Leave the chicken to cool in the stock at room temperature for about 30 minutes, then transfer the chicken and stock to a bowl, cover with cling film and refrigerate until cold.

2. To prepare the salad, bring a large saucepan of water to the boil over medium-high heat. Add the noodles and boil until tender but still chewy, about 3 minutes or according to the packet directions.

3. Put the bean sprouts in the sieve you will use to drain the noodles. Pour the pan of noodles over the bean sprouts to drain, wilting the bean sprouts in the process. Rinse well under cold running water to cool the noodles and sprouts, then drain well.

Transfer the noodles and sprouts to a large mixing bowl. Add the spring onions, cucumber, carrot and coriander. Tear the chicken into thin, bite-size shreds and add it to the bowl, reserving the stock for another use, if you wish. Toss the ingredients lightly to combine them.

4. Prepare the dressing. In a small mixing bowl, stir together the sesame paste, rice vinegar, soy sauce, ginger and sugar; they will form a fairly thick paste. Little by little, stir in enough of the hot water to thin the paste to a smooth creamy consistency.

Pour the dressing over the salad mixture and toss well to coat all the ingredients.

5. Arrange the spinach leaves to form beds on large individual serving plates or bowls. Mound the salad on top of the spinach and garnish with coriander sprigs.

TEST KITCHEN NOTES

NOODLE MIXTURES LIKE THIS—CALLED *DAN DAN MEIN* OR SOME PHONETIC VARIATION ON THAT—CAN BE FOUND IN SOME CHINESE RESTAURANTS. THE DISH MAKES A SPECTACULAR, FILLING MAIN COURSE SALAD FOR A WARM WEATHER LUNCH OR DINNER.

IF YOU DON'T HAVE ANY CHINESE NOODLES, YOU CAN SUBSTITUTE LINGUINE OR SPAGHETTI, WHICH WILL WORK PERFECTLY WELL HERE.

Italian Steak Salad with Rocket, Gorgonzola and Balsamic Vinaigrette

SERVES 4

STEAK

1 x 675g (1½lb) piece rump steak, trimmed of visible fat

1 garlic clove, cut in half

2 tablespoons balsamic vinegar

2 tablespoons extra virgin olive oil

Salt

Black pepper

DRESSING

4 tablespoons balsamic vinegar

¼ teaspoon salt

¼ teaspoon black pepper

½ teaspoon Dijon mustard

125ml (4fl oz) extra virgin olive oil

SALAD

225g (8oz) rocket leaves

1 red pepper, roasted, peeled and seeded (see pages 15–16), then torn into thin strips

175g (6oz) Gorgonzola cheese

25g (1oz) pine nuts, toasted (see page 17)

1. First, marinate the steak. Rub it lightly all over with the cut sides of the garlic. In a bowl just large enough to hold the meat, stir together the balsamic vinegar and olive oil. Turn the steak in the marinade to coat it well and leave at room temperature for about 30 minutes.

2. Preheat the grill.

3. Prepare the dressing. In a small mixing bowl, use a fork or small wire whisk to stir together the vinegar, salt and pepper until the salt dissolves. Add the mustard and stir until thoroughly blended. Stirring continuously, pour in the oil in a thin, steady stream. Set the dressing aside.

4. Season the steak generously all over with salt and black pepper. Grill until done to your liking, about 2 minutes per side for medium-rare.

5. While the steak cooks, put the rocket leaves and pepper strips in a mixing bowl and, tossing continuously, pour in enough of the dressing to coat them to your liking. Arrange the salad mixture in mounds on large individual serving plates.

6. As soon as the steak is done, carve it crossways and diagonally into slices no thicker than 5mm (¼in), immediately draping the slices over the mounds of salad so the meat's juices will mingle with the dressing. Crumble the Gorgonzola over the steak and salad, garnish with pine nuts and serve immediately.

TEST KITCHEN NOTES

I FIRST ENJOYED A SALAD SIMILAR TO THIS AT A FAVOURITE ITALIAN TRATTORIA SEVERAL YEARS AGO AND I'VE BEEN TINKERING WITH THE CONCEPT EVER SINCE. SEVERAL FACTORS ARE CENTRAL TO MAKING IT MORE THAN JUST A SLAB OF MEAT SERVED ON A PILE OF GREENS. FIRST, MARINATING THE MEAT WITH BALSAMIC VINEGAR AND OLIVE OIL SUBTLY TIES ITS TASTE TO THAT OF THE DRESSING. SECOND, THE CHOICE OF PEPPERY ROCKET, HIGHLIGHTED BY SWEET STRIPS OF ROASTED PEPPER, STANDS UP WELL TO THE MEAT'S ROBUST FLAVOUR. FINALLY, GRILLING THE STEAK JUST MOMENTS BEFORE SERVING AND PLACING THE SLICES ON TOP OF THE GREENS WHILE STILL DRIPPING WITH HOT JUICES, ALLOWS THE FLAVOURS TO MINGLE WONDERFULLY.

Oven-fried Chicken on Pickled Vegetable Coleslaw with Bacon and Pecans

SERVES 4

OVEN-FRIED CHICKEN

175ml (6fl oz) buttermilk

1 teaspoon salt

¼ teaspoon black pepper

⅛ teaspoon paprika

4 drops Tabasco sauce

4 large boneless, skinless chicken
    breasts, about 175g (6oz) each

25g (1oz) cornflakes, finely crushed

Pinch cayenne pepper

DRESSING

4 tablespoons cider vinegar

1 teaspoon celery seeds

2 teaspoons caster sugar

½ teaspoon salt

½ teaspoon white pepper

6 tablespoons walnut oil or vegetable oil

SALAD

½ red cabbage

½ green cabbage

2 carrots, coarsely grated

4 whole sweet pickled cucumbers,
    coarsely grated

2 tablespoons finely chopped
    fresh flat-leaf parsley

2 tablespoons finely chopped
    fresh chives

225g (8oz) smoked streaky bacon, thinly
    sliced

350g (12oz) round lettuce

85g (3oz) pecan pieces or halves,
    toasted (see page 17)

Parsley sprigs, for garnish

1. To make the chicken, pour the buttermilk into a mixing bowl and stir in half each of the salt, pepper and paprika and all of the Tabasco sauce. Trim any traces of fat from the chicken breasts and add them to the bowl, turning them in the buttermilk to coat completely. Cover the bowl with cling film and refrigerate for at least 1 hour and preferably several hours; turn the chicken breasts several times during soaking.

2. When you are ready to cook the chicken, preheat the oven to 190°C (375°F, gas mark 5). Select a baking dish large enough to hold the chicken breasts comfortably in a single layer and spray the inside of the dish with non-stick cooking spray or brush with oil. On a dinner plate or in a shallow bowl placed next to the baking dish, stir together the crushed cornflakes and remaining seasonings, spreading them out in an even bed. One at a time, lift each chicken breast from the buttermilk and, with your fingertips, turn it in the cornflake mixture to coat it completely and evenly, then place it gently in the baking dish.

When all the chicken breasts have been coated, cover the baking dish with foil and put it in the preheated oven. Cook the chicken, covered, for 20 minutes, then remove the foil and continue cooking until the coating has evenly browned, about 20 minutes more. Remove the chicken and leave to cool to room temperature. Refrigerate until serving time.

3. While the chicken is cooking, prepare the dressing and the slaw. For the dressing, in a mixing bowl, use a fork or a small wire whisk to stir together the cider vinegar, celery seeds, sugar, salt and white pepper until the sugar and salt dissolve. Stirring briskly, pour in the oil in a thin, steady stream. Set the dressing aside.

4. Fill a kettle with water and bring it to the boil over medium-high heat. Meanwhile, cut the cabbage halves in half again to make quarters and cut out their cores. Place each wedge cut side down on a cutting surface and, with a sharp knife, slice it very thinly to make shreds. Layer the shreds in a large colander or sieve: first the red cabbage, then the green, then the grated carrot. When the water reaches the boil, hold the colander or sieve over the sink and pour the boiling water slowly and evenly over the vegetables to wilt them. Drain well.

Transfer the wilted vegetables to a large mixing bowl. Add the grated pickles, the parsley and the chives. Pour the dressing in and toss thoroughly. Cover the bowl with cling film and refrigerate until serving time.

5. To cook the bacon, arrange the rashers side by side in one or two frying pans and cook over medium heat, turning frequently, until crisp and brown, about 10 minutes. Remove the bacon and set aside to drain on several layers of kitchen paper towel.

6. To serve the salad, arrange the lettuce leaves on large, chilled individual serving plates. Mound the pickled vegetable slaw on each bed of lettuce. Crumble or chop the bacon and scatter over the slaw. For each serving, slice a chicken breast crossways into pieces 1cm (½in) thick and arrange them on top of the slaw. Garnish with the pecans and parsley sprigs.

Greek Country-style Lamb Salad

SERVES 4

DRESSING

4 tablespoons lemon juice

¼ teaspoon salt

¼ teaspoon black pepper

⅛ teaspoon caster sugar

125ml (4fl oz) extra virgin olive oil

SALAD

85g (3oz) dried small pasta shells

4 plum tomatoes, cored and cut into
    1cm (½in) chunks

1 cucumber, halved lengthways, seeded
    and halves cut crossways into 1cm
    (½in) thick slices

1 green pepper, halved, seeded and cut
    into 1cm (½in) chunks

1 red pepper, halved, seeded and cut
    into 1cm (½in) chunks

½ small red onion, cut into 3mm (⅛in) dice

450g (1lb) cooked lamb, cut into thin
    bite-size slices

225g (8oz) feta cheese, crumbled

175g (6oz) black olives, pitted

2 tablespoons fresh oregano leaves,
    finely chopped, or 1 tablespoon
    dried oregano, crumbled

225g (8oz) baby salad leaves

4 fresh oregano or parsley sprigs,
    for garnish

1. To make the dressing, put the lemon juice in a small mixing bowl. Add the salt, pepper and sugar and, with a fork or small whisk, stir until the salt and sugar dissolve. Stirring continuously, pour in the olive oil until blended. Set the dressing aside.

2. Bring a saucepan of water to the boil. Add the pasta shells and boil until tender but still slightly chewy, 8 to 10 minutes or according to the suggested time in the packet instructions. Drain the pasta in a sieve, rinse well under cold running water and drain again.

Put the pasta in a large mixing bowl and add the tomatoes, cucumber, peppers, onion, lamb, feta, olives and oregano. Add the dressing and toss well to coat the ingredients.

3. Arrange the leaves on large, chilled individual serving plates or bowls. Distribute the salad mixture equally among the four beds of leaves and garnish with sprigs of oregano or parsley.

Moroccan Grilled Lamb Salad with Couscous and Dried Fruit

SERVES 4

DRESSING

5 tablespoons lemon juice
½ tablespoon honey
2 tablespoons finely chopped fresh mint
   leaves
150ml (¼pint) extra virgin olive oil

SALAD

450g (1lb) lamb
1 teaspoon vegetable oil
1 teaspoon ground cumin
½ teaspoon ground cinnamon
¼ teaspoon salt
¼ teaspoon black pepper
225g (8oz) dried mixed fruit, such as
   apricots and seedless raisins
450ml (16fl oz) water
325g (11oz) quick-cooking couscous
115g (4oz) stoned dates, coarsely
   chopped
55g (2oz) flaked almonds, toasted
   (see page 17)
350g (12oz) spinach or other medium-
   size tender salad leaves, thoroughly
   washed
Fresh mint sprigs, for garnish

1. To make the dressing, put the lemon juice in a small mixing bowl, add the honey and stir with a fork or small whisk until the honey dissolves. Stir in the mint. Stirring continuously, slowly add the olive oil. Set the dressing aside.

2. To make the salad, first marinate the lamb. In a shallow dish large enough to hold the lamb, stir together the oil, cumin, cinnamon, salt and pepper to form a paste. Rub this paste all over the lamb and leave it to marinate at room temperature for 15 to 30 minutes.

3. Meanwhile, preheat the grill or barbecue.

4. While the lamb is marinating, put the dried fruit, excluding the dates, in a bowl and add enough hot water to cover them. Leave them to soak until tender, about 10 minutes. Drain well, cut any large pieces into thin strips and set aside.

5. In a medium saucepan, bring the water to the boil over medium-high heat. Stir in the couscous, cover the pan, remove it from the heat and leave for about 5 minutes, until the couscous is tender. With a fork, gently fluff the couscous, then transfer it to a large mixing bowl. Add the dried fruit, dates and almonds and toss gently but thoroughly to combine. Set aside.

6. Grill or barbecue the lamb until done to your liking, 3 to 4 minutes per side for medium-rare.

7. While the lamb is cooking, arrange the spinach or other salad leaves to form attractive beds on individual large serving plates. Mound the couscous mixture in the centre of each plate.

8. Cut the lamb crossways into 5mm–1cm (¼–½in) thick slices and arrange them on top of the couscous. Garnish with mint sprigs and serve immediately.

TEST KITCHEN NOTES

COUSCOUS IS A FORM OF TINY PASTA PELLETS MADE FROM SEMOLINA WHEAT FLOUR. IN ITS TRADITIONAL FORM, THIS NORTH AFRICAN SPECIALITY CAN TAKE QUITE A WHILE TO PREPARE, REQUIRING SLOW STEAMING OVER SIMMERING WATER OR STOCK. THIS RECIPE TAKES ADVANTAGE OF THE QUICK-COOKING VARIETY OF COUSCOUS, WHICH CAN BE PREPARED IN JUST A FEW MINUTES.

TOSS IN WHATEVER KINDS OF DRIED FRUIT AND NUTS YOU LIKE WITH THE COUSCOUS AND DRESSING. FOR EVEN MORE FLAVOUR, YOU COULD USE A LITTLE APPLE JUICE OR SOME WHITE WINE, GENTLY HEATED IN A SMALL SAUCEPAN, TO SOFTEN THE FRUITS.

Grilled Tandoori Chicken Salad

SERVES 4

DRESSING

6 tablespoons plain low-fat yogurt

6 tablespoons mayonnaise

25g (1oz) sweet mango chutney, large
    pieces of fruit finely chopped

2 tablespoons lemon juice

½ teaspoon salt

½ teaspoon white pepper

SALAD

175g (6oz) plain low-fat yogurt

2 teaspoons curry powder

1 teaspoon finely grated fresh root
    ginger

½ tablespoon lemon juice

4 boneless, skinless chicken breasts,
    115–175g (4–6oz) each

2 large potatoes, 175g (6oz) each

1 tablespoon vegetable oil

Salt

White pepper

675g (1½lb) mixed bitter salad greens
    such as rocket, radicchio, escarole
    and chicory

4 plum tomatoes, cut into wedges

1 small red onion, thinly sliced

40g (1½oz) sultanas

25g (1oz) cashew nuts, toasted (see page
    17)

15g (½oz) fresh coriander leaves,
    finely chopped

1. To prepare the dressing, stir together all the ingredients in a small mixing bowl. Cover the bowl with cling film and refrigerate.

2. To begin preparing the salad, put the yogurt, curry powder, ginger and lemon juice in a shallow dish large enough to hold the chicken breasts in a single layer. Stir well to blend, then add the chicken breasts and turn to coat them well. Leave to marinate for 15 to 30 minutes.

3. Meanwhile, preheat the grill or barbecue.

4. At the same time, cut the potatoes into 1cm (½in) thick slices and put them in a medium-size saucepan. Add cold water to cover and put the pan over medium-high heat. As soon as the water reaches a boil, drain well.

5. Brush the potato slices with the vegetable oil. Season the chicken breasts and potatoes with salt and white pepper to taste. Grill or barbecue the chicken and the potatoes until both are golden brown and the chicken is cooked through, about 5 minutes per side.

6. While the chicken and potatoes are cooking, arrange the salad leaves in beds on large individual serving plates. Cut the chicken breasts crossways into 1cm (½in) wide pieces and arrange one on each salad. Place the potato slices and tomato wedges around the chicken. Separate the onion slices into rings and place them over each salad.

7. Stir the dressing briefly, then drizzle it over each salad. Garnish with sultanas, cashews and coriander and serve immediately.

TEST KITCHEN NOTES

TANDOORI CHICKEN IS AN INDIAN SPECIALITY IN WHICH CHICKEN PIECES ARE MARINATED IN SPICED YOGURT, THEN COOKED IN A CHARCOAL-FIRED TANDOOR OVEN. USUALLY, INDIAN RESTAURANTS SERVE THE CHICKEN ON A PLATTER GARNISHED WITH LETTUCE, SLICED ONION AND WEDGES OF TOMATO AND LEMON, WHICH STRIKES ME AS MORE THAN HALFWAY TO BEING A SALAD.

THIS DELIGHTFUL RECIPE TAKES THE CONCEPT THE REST OF THE WAY, WHILE APPROXIMATING TANDOORI CHICKEN'S TENDERNESS, SUCCULENCE AND SUBTLE SPICE WITHOUT THE USE OF A TANDOOR. THE SAME CURRY TREATMENT ALSO WORKS PERFECTLY WELL WITH LARGE RAW PRAWNS OR WITH THIN SLICES OF LAMB FILLET.

Sautéed Mushroom Salad with Goat's Cheese and Sun-dried Tomatoes

SERVES 4

675g (1½lb) mixed baby salad leaves

12 dry-packed sun-dried tomatoes

6 tablespoons extra virgin olive oil

4 shallots, finely chopped

675g (1½lb) mixed mushrooms, tough stalks removed and discarded, caps and tender stalks cut into 1cm (½in) thick slices

Salt

Black pepper

4 tablespoons sherry vinegar or balsamic vinegar

6 tablespoons walnut oil

115g (4oz) fresh, creamy goat's cheese

25g (1oz) Parmesan cheese, freshly grated (optional)

55g (2oz) walnuts, toasted (see page 17)

15g (½oz) fresh chives or basil, finely chopped

1. Arrange the salad leaves on large individual serving plates.

2. Put the sun-dried tomatoes in a small bowl and add hot water to cover. Leave them to soak for about 10 minutes, until tender, then drain well and cut the pieces into 5mm (¼in) wide strips. Set aside.

3. In a large frying pan, heat the olive oil over high heat. Add the shallots and, as soon as they sizzle, add the mushrooms. Sauté them, stirring continuously and briskly with a wooden spoon, until they are heated through and their edges begin to brown, 2 to 3 minutes. Stir in the sun-dried tomato pieces and season generously to taste with salt and pepper.

Add the vinegar to the frying pan and stir and scrape to deglaze any pan sediment. Stir in the walnut oil.

4. Immediately spoon the mushrooms, sun-dried tomatoes and hot pan dressing over the salad leaves. Crumble the goat's cheese and scatter over each salad. Sprinkle with the walnuts and chives or basil. Serve immediately.

TEST KITCHEN NOTES

As a lifelong lover of mushrooms, I continue to be amazed by the ever-increasing availability of varieties we once termed 'wild mushrooms'. Consider what you might find in a well-stocked supermarket or green-grocer's: trumpet-shaped, yolk-yellow chanterelles; round, meaty-textured, dark-brown shiitake mushrooms, a speciality of Japan; delicate oyster mushrooms, whose colour, shape and taste recall that briny shellfish; big, open brown field mushrooms, the closest the mushroom world comes to a steak; and the chestnut mushroom, which looks like the sun-tanned cousin of the familiar cultivated button mushroom.

The more of these mushrooms you can find and include in this salad, the more delightful it will be. (Although, I daresay, it would still taste terrific if all you can find are button mushrooms.) Quickly sautéed with shallots in olive oil, then deglazed with sherry vinegar and scented with walnut oil to make their own warm pan dressing, the mushrooms are spooned over baby greens and finished with crumbled goat's cheese that will begin to melt as you bring the salad to the table.

Bruschetta Tomato Salad with Parma Ham and Mozzarella

SERVES 4

TOMATO SALAD

16 plum tomatoes

1 large shallot, finely chopped

125ml (4fl oz) extra virgin olive oil

4 tablespoons balsamic vinegar

15g (½oz) fresh flat-leaf parsley, finely chopped

¾ teaspoon salt

½ teaspoon black pepper

25g (1oz) fresh basil leaves, finely shredded

BRUSCHETTA

32 slices ciabatta, cut diagonally 1cm (½in) thick

175ml (6fl oz) extra virgin olive oil

115g (4oz) Parma ham, very thinly sliced

450g (1lb) fresh mozzarella, thinly sliced

1. To make the tomato salad, first core the tomatoes and cut them in half crossways. With a fingertip, scoop out and discard the seeds from each tomato half. Coarsely chop the tomatoes and put them in a mixing bowl. Add the shallot, olive oil, vinegar, parsley, salt and pepper and toss well. Cover with cling film and marinate in the refrigerator for about 1 hour.

2. Prepare the bruschetta shortly before serving time. Preheat the grill or barbecue. Brush the bread slices on both sides with the olive oil and toast them until golden brown, 2 to 3 minutes per side. If using a barbecue, distribute the Parma ham and then the cheese evenly over the slices immediately after you turn them over, so the cheese will melt while you toast the undersides. If using a grill, toast the bread slices on both sides, then remove them from the grill, top with the Parma ham and cheese and return them briefly to the grill until the cheese melts, about 1 minute more.

3. Arrange the bruschetta, cheese side up, on large individual serving plates. Spoon the tomato salad generously on top of each bruschetta and garnish with the basil. Serve immediately.

TEST KITCHEN NOTES

THE ITALIAN HORS D'OEUVRE OF TOASTED BREAD TOPPED WITH ANY NUMBER OF SAVOURY INGREDIENTS HAS BECOME VERY FASHIONABLE IN RECENT YEARS. IN ITS MOST POPULAR FORM, THE BREAD IS SIMPLY RUBBED WITH GARLIC AND OLIVE OIL BEFORE BEING GRILLED OR BARBECUED, AND IS THEN TOPPED WITH A FRAGRANT MIXTURE OF SUN-RIPENED TOMATOES, GARLIC, HERBS AND A VINAIGRETTE DRESSING.

IF YOU TAKE THE SAME BASIC ELEMENTS, CUBE THE BREAD AND TOSS IT TOGETHER WITH THE TOMATOES, YOU GET AN ITALIAN COUNTRY-STYLE SALAD KNOWN AS *PANZANELLA*. CONSIDERING THAT A GOOD BRUSCHETTA CAN OFTEN BE THE MOST MEMORABLE PART OF MANY AN ITALIAN MEAL, IT MAKES SENSE, THEN, TO TURN IT INTO A MAIN MEAL SALAD.

Spinach and Goat's Cheese Salad with Dried Fruit and Warm Honey-Mustard Vinaigrette

SERVES 4

DRESSING

125ml (4fl oz) balsamic vinegar

2 tablespoons dried cherries

8 dried apricots, cut into 3mm (⅛in) wide slivers

1 teaspoon Dijon mustard

1 teaspoon honey

125ml (4fl oz) extra virgin olive oil

SALAD

675g (1½lb) baby spinach leaves, thoroughly washed

450g (1lb) fresh, creamy goat's cheese, divided into 8 equal rounds

4 tablespoons extra virgin olive oil

Salt

White pepper

55g (2oz) pecans, toasted (see page 17)

2 tablespoons finely chopped fresh chives

1. To begin making the dressing, put the vinegar in a small saucepan and heat it over medium heat until bubbles begin to appear round the edges. Remove the pan from the heat, add the dried cherries and apricots, cover and leave them to soak for 10 minutes.

Remove the fruits with a slotted spoon and set them aside. With a small fork or wire whisk, stir the mustard and honey into the pan of vinegar until blended. Stirring continuously over medium-low heat, pour in the oil in a thin, steady stream. Remove from the heat, return the dried fruit to the dressing and cover the pan.

2. Preheat the grill.

3. To prepare the salad, arrange the spinach leaves on large individual serving plates.

4. Line a shallow baking dish large enough to hold all the cheese rounds with foil. Lightly coat each goat's cheese round all over with some olive oil and place it on the foil. Sprinkle the cheese rounds lightly with salt and white pepper.

Put the cheese rounds under the grill, keeping a close eye on them and removing them as soon as they begin to show signs of bubbling and melting, 1 to 2 minutes.

With a spatula, transfer 2 cheese rounds to each bed of spinach. With a large spoon, drizzle the warm dressing and dried fruit evenly over the cheese and spinach. Garnish with pecans and chives. Serve immediately.

TEST KITCHEN NOTES

THIS HEARTY SALAD EXPLODES WITH WONDERFULLY HEADY AROMAS AND FLAVOURS: THE TANGY RICHNESS OF THE BUBBLING-HOT GOAT'S CHEESE, THE INTENSE FRUITINESS OF DRIED CHERRIES AND APRICOTS SOAKED IN BALSAMIC VINEGAR, AND THE SWEET-SPICY TASTE OF THE WARM HONEY-MUSTARD DRESSING.

BUY A GOOD, FRESH, CREAMY GOAT'S CHEESE SHAPED INTO A LOG THAT YOU CAN NEATLY CUT INTO ROUNDS. DEPENDING ON THE BRAND, YOU MIGHT ACTUALLY HAVE TO BUY TWO OR MORE SEPARATE CHEESES TO GET THE REQUIRED AMOUNT.

IF DRIED CHERRIES ARE UNAVAILABLE, SUBSTITUTE SEEDLESS RAISINS.

Grilled Pork and Fresh Fig Salad

SERVES 4

DRESSING

4 tablespoons sherry vinegar

½ teaspoon salt

½ teaspoon caster sugar

¼ teaspoon black pepper

4 tablespoons hazelnut or walnut oil

4 tablespoons vegetable oil

SALAD

350g (12oz) pork fillet, cut into
   1cm (½in) thick medallions

1 tablespoon sherry vinegar

1 tablespoon hazelnut or walnut oil

Salt

Black pepper

12 fresh, ripe figs

450g (1lb) baby spinach leaves,
   thoroughly washed

115g (4oz) fresh, creamy goat's cheese

85g (3oz) hazelnuts, toasted (see page
   17), skinned and coarsely chopped

1. To make the dressing, put the sherry vinegar in a small mixing bowl. Add the salt, sugar and pepper and use a fork or small whisk to stir until the salt and sugar dissolve. Stirring continuously, slowly pour in the hazelnut or walnut oil and the vegetable oil. Set the dressing aside.

2. Put the pork medallions in a small bowl and drizzle them with the tablespoon each of sherry vinegar and hazelnut or walnut oil. Turn the medallions to coat them well and leave to marinate at room temperature for about 15 minutes.

3. Meanwhile, preheat the grill or barbecue. When it is hot, season the pork with salt and pepper and cook until medium to medium-well done, 4 to 5 minutes per side. When you turn the pork over, brush the figs all over with some of the dressing and cook them alongside the pork, turning them frequently to brown evenly.

4. When the pork and figs are done, remove them from the heat. Toss the spinach with enough of the remaining dressing to coat well and arrange it on four large individual serving plates or shallow bowls. With a small, sharp knife, cut each fig lengthways into quarters. Arrange the pork medallions and figs on top of the spinach. Crumble the goat's cheese over each salad and garnish with the hazelnuts. Serve immediately.

TEST KITCHEN NOTES

I FIND PORK TO BE A DELIGHTFULLY ROBUST MEAT WITH AN INHERENT SWEETNESS AND A RICHNESS OF TASTE THAT MAKES IT AN IDEAL CANDIDATE FOR THE STARRING ROLE IN THIS HEARTY MAIN MEAL SALAD.

TO GO WITH THE PORK, I CHOSE SUITABLY FULL-FLAVOURED INGREDIENTS: SPINACH, GOAT'S CHEESE, TOASTED HAZELNUTS AND, MOST IMPORTANT, FRESH FIGS.

YOU CAN FIND FRESH FIGS IN WELL-STOCKED SUPERMARKETS AND GREENGROCERS' FROM EARLY SUMMER WELL INTO AUTUMN. SELECT ONES THAT ARE FULLY RIPE, PLUMP AND TENDER TO THE TOUCH AND THAT HAVE A SWEET AROMA SUGGESTING A COMMENSURATE SWEETNESS OF TASTE. BRIEF GRILLING OF THE FIGS ONLY FURTHER EMPHASISES THAT NATURAL SWEETNESS BY SLIGHTLY CARAMELISING THE SUGAR IN THE OUTERMOST LAYER OF THE FRUIT.

YOU MAY FIND, AS I HAVE, THAT THE FIGS ARE SO SEDUCTIVE AND GO SO WELL WITH THE NUTS AND CHEESE THAT THEY CAN TAKE OVER THE LEAD IN THE SALAD. IF YOU WISH TO LEAVE OUT THE PORK, INCREASE THE QUANTITY OF FIGS BY HALF.

The Baked Potato Salad

SERVES 4

DRESSING

Ranch Dressing (see page 26)

SALAD

4 large baking potatoes
2 tablespoons extra virgin olive oil
Salt
Black pepper
2 medium courgettes, trimmed and
    coarsely grated
2 medium carrots, trimmed and coarsely
    grated
1 red pepper, quartered, seeded and
    quarters cut crossways into thin
    strips
175g (6oz) cooked or canned palm
    hearts, peeled and coarsely grated
115g (4oz) mushrooms, thinly sliced
15g (½oz) fresh basil, finely shredded or
    finely chopped fresh chives

1. Prepare the Ranch Dressing and set aside.

2. Preheat the oven to 190°C (375°F, gas mark 5).

3. Rinse the potatoes and lightly scrub them to remove any dirt. Dry them well with a tea towel or kitchen paper towel. In a shallow dish, roll the potatoes all over in the olive oil. Sprinkle them generously to taste with salt and pepper.

Place a sheet of foil just big enough to hold the potatoes on the centre rack of the oven. Put the potatoes on the foil, not touching each other and bake until they feel tender when squeezed with an oven glove and their skins are nicely browned and crisp.

Remove the potatoes from the oven and put each in a large, shallow serving bowl or individual serving plate. With a small, sharp knife, cut a lengthways slit deep into the top of each potato. Protecting your hands with a folded tea towel, squeeze each potato, pushing inwards from both ends, to open it wide. With two forks, spread the potato open to make a big, generous cavity.

4. In a mixing bowl, toss together the prepared raw vegetables. Stuff them into each potato, allowing the vegetables to overflow. Drizzle the dressing generously over each serving and garnish with basil or chives. Serve immediately.

TEST KITCHEN NOTES

ONE EVENING DURING THE MONTHS WHILE I WAS DEVELOPING THE RECIPES FOR THIS BOOK, I SELECTED A BIG BAKED POTATO, SPLIT IT OPEN AND STARTED PILING ON TOP OF IT ALL SORTS OF GRATED AND SLICED RAW VEGETABLES. THEN, I DRIZZLED EVERYTHING WITH TANGY RANCH DRESSING, WHICH SEEMED THE PERFECT COMPLEMENT TO BOTH THE SALAD AND THE POTATO.

WHAT YOU WILL BE DOING HERE IS USING THE POTATO AS THE SALAD BOWL.

TAKE THE RECIPE HERE AS A BASIC FORMULA. SUBSTITUTE ANY OTHER FRESH, RAW VEGETABLES THAT APPEAL TO YOU, SLICING OR GRATING THEM IN SUCH A WAY THAT THEY CAN BE STUFFED EASILY INTO THE BAKED POTATOES AND EATEN WITH A FORK. ADD SOME GRATED OR CRUMBLED CHEESE OF YOUR CHOICE. IF YOU WANT AN EVEN RICHER TOPPING, SUBSTITUTE CLASSIC BLUE CHEESE DRESSING (SEE PAGE 25) FOR THE RANCH.

Grilled Vegetable Salad with Goat's Cheese and Pine Nuts

SERVES 4

DRESSING

125ml (4fl oz) balsamic vinegar

½ teaspoon salt

½ teaspoon pepper

175ml (6fl oz) extra virgin olive oil

SALAD

4 medium courgettes, preferably 2 green and 2 yellow, cut lengthways into 5mm (¼in) thick slices

4 plum tomatoes, cored and halved lengthways

1 sweet white or red onion, cut crossways into 1cm (½in) thick slices

1 red pepper, quartered, cored and seeded, each quarter gently flattened

12 large open mushrooms, stalks trimmed even with caps

675g (1½lb) mixed baby salad leaves

85g (3oz) fresh, creamy goat's cheese

25g (1oz) pine nuts, toasted (see page 17)

15g (½oz) fresh basil leaves, finely shredded

1. First make the dressing. In a small mixing bowl, use a fork or small wire whisk to stir together the vinegar, salt and pepper until the salt dissolves. Stirring continuously, slowly pour in the olive oil.

2. Pour 125ml (4fl oz) of the dressing into a shallow dish large enough to hold all the sliced and whole vegetables comfortably. Add the vegetables and turn to coat them evenly with the dressing. Leave them to marinate while you pre-heat the grill or barbecue.

3. Grill or barbecue all the vegetables until nicely browned, about 4 minutes per side.

4. While the vegetables are cooking, put the salad leaves in a large mixing bowl and toss them with the remaining dressing until evenly coated. Arrange the leaves on large individual serving plates.

5. As soon as the vegetables are done, arrange them on top of each salad. Crumble the goat's cheese over the vegetables. Garnish with pine nuts and basil. Serve immediately.

TEST KITCHEN NOTES

To me, this salad captures all the glory of fresh summer produce: crisp, tender greens coated with a simple, clean-tasting dressing; succulent vegetables, their flavours intensified by marinating them in the dressing and then grilling or barbecuing them; and hints of fresh goat's cheese, pine nuts and basil to add a little richness to the experience.

It is interesting how robust the results can be. You can make it even more so, while still retaining its vegetarian character, by grilling a few thick slices of parboiled waxy potato. By all means add to the salad any other vegetables that seem appropriate and look good, including small heads of radicchio or chicory, halved lengthways; parboiled slices of sweet potato; pieces of corn on the cob; whole spring onions; and even lengthways slices of carrot or parsnip, which develop a wonderfully rich sweetness as the intense heat caramelises their natural sugars.

CHAPTER 6

Light and Refreshing Salads

Just because a salad is light and refreshing doesn't mean it can't still make a satisfying meal. Witness the main meal salads on the pages that follow: combinations of fresh fruit with vibrant-tasting dressings or dips; platefuls of delicate vegetables and seafood; cool cucumber salads topped with zestily flavoured poultry; salads of pasta garnished with all manner of tempting titbits.

Each of these salads, and more besides, are bound to bring you satisfaction—not necessarily by filling you up until you can't eat another bite or by chasing away the chill, as do some of the other salads in this book, but by making your taste buds stand to attention and by wafting across your palate like a fresh tropical breeze. Through their imaginative use of seasonings, their sometimes unconventional combinations of ingredients, their often strict attention to seasonality and—sometimes, yes—their sheer audacity, they offer you sensations the likes of which you probably have not enjoyed before. Now that's satisfaction indeed.

Sesame-crusted Salmon Salad

SERVES 4

DRESSING

4 tablespoons rice vinegar
½ teaspoon salt
½ teaspoon caster sugar
¼ teaspoon white pepper
2 tablespoons toasted sesame oil

SALAD

450g (1lb) fresh salmon fillet, cut into 4
    equal pieces
6 tablespoons yellow *miso* paste
2 tablespoons soy sauce
2 teaspoons finely grated fresh
    root ginger
55–85g (2–3oz) sesame seeds
675g (1½lb) baby spinach leaves,
    thoroughly washed
25g (1oz) pickled pink ginger

1. To make the dressing, stir together the rice vinegar, salt, sugar and pepper in a small mixing bowl until the salt and sugar dissolve. Stirring continuously, slowly pour in the sesame oil. Set the dressing aside.

2. Place each salmon fillet piece flat on a cutting board. With a sharp knife, carefully butterfly each fillet by cutting it horizontally but not completely in half, opening it out to a piece twice its original dimensions and half its original thickness.

3. In a large, shallow dish or bowl, stir together the *miso*, soy sauce and ginger. Turn the butterflied salmon fillets in this mixture to coat them evenly.

4. Preheat the grill. Line a baking dish or baking sheet large enough to hold all the butterflied fillets with foil. Coat it lightly with non-stick cooking spray or brush with oil.

5. As soon as the grill is hot, spread the sesame seeds evenly on a plate or other flat surface larger than one butterflied salmon piece. Gently turn each salmon piece in the sesame seeds to coat it evenly, then transfer it to the foil-lined baking dish.

Grill the salmon until it is just cooked through and the sesame crust is golden brown, 3 to 4 minutes per side.

6. While the salmon is grilling, toss the spinach leaves with the reserved dressing and arrange them on large serving plates. Use a fish slice to carefully transfer each salmon fillet next to a bed of spinach. Top the salmon with pickled ginger and serve immediately.

TEST KITCHEN NOTES

ALTHOUGH THE CONCEPT OF COATING SALMON FILLETS WITH A SESAME SEED CRUST MIGHT SOUND COMPLICATED, IT IS IN FACT QUITE EASY, MAKING THIS SALAD IDEAL TO PREPARE FOR AN ELEGANT DINNER PARTY AT WHICH YOU WANT TO SERVE YOUR GUESTS SOMETHING LIGHT BUT SATISFYING AND MEMORABLE.

THE ONLY INGREDIENTS WITH WHICH YOU MIGHT NOT BE FAMILIAR—NAMELY RICE VINEGAR, YELLOW *MISO* (SOYA BEAN PASTE) AND PICKLED PINK GINGER—ARE AVAILABLE IN SOME WELL-STOCKED SUPERMARKETS AS WELL AS JAPANESE DELIS. IF YOU CAN'T FIND THE GINGER, SUBSTITUTE THIN SLICES OF LEMON.

FOR THE SALMON, BUY FILLETS CUT FROM THE CENTRE OF THE FISH, WHICH WILL GIVE YOU FAIRLY THICK, UNIFORM PIECES. BEFORE PREPARING THE SALMON, FEEL THE SURFACE OF EACH PIECE WITH YOUR FINGERTIPS IN SEARCH OF ANY ERRANT LITTLE BONES, THEN GRASP THEM BETWEEN YOUR FINGERTIPS OR WITH A PAIR OF TWEEZERS AND PULL THEM OUT.

Smoked Salmon and New Potato Salad with Crème Fraîche and Fines Herbes

SERVES 4

900g (2lb) new potatoes, lightly rinsed
    of any dirt
225g (8oz) crème fraîche
25g (1oz) finely chopped red onion
1½ tablespoons lemon juice
1 tablespoon finely grated lemon zest
1 tablespoon finely chopped fresh chives
1 tablespoon finely snipped fresh dill
1 tablespoon finely chopped fresh
    flat-leaf parsley
Salt
Black pepper
225g (8oz) mixed baby salad greens
450g (1lb) smoked salmon, thinly sliced
2 lemons, cut into wedges
25g (1oz) salmon caviar (optional)

1. Put the potatoes in a saucepan of lightly salted water. Bring to the boil over medium-high heat and cook until the potatoes are tender when pierced with the tip of a small, sharp knife, about 10 minutes.

Drain the potatoes well and rinse several times in cold water until they are just cool enough to handle. With a knife, quarter each potato, dropping it into a mixing bowl. Add the crème fraîche, red onion, lemon juice and zest, chives, dill and parsley. With a spoon, gently mix the ingredients together until the crème fraîche evenly coats the potatoes. Season generously to taste with salt and pepper and gently mix again.

2. Arrange the salad leaves on large, chilled individual serving plates. Mound the potato salad on each plate. Loosely roll up the smoked salmon slices and drape them over the potatoes on each plate. Nestle lemon wedges nearby for guests to squeeze over their servings. If you like, garnish the salmon with spoonsful of salmon caviar.

TEST KITCHEN NOTES

MAKE THIS SALAD WHEN SPRINGTIME'S TENDER LITTLE NEW POTATOES ARE AVAILABLE AND WHEN YOU CAN LAY YOUR HANDS ON SOME REALLY GOOD SMOKED SALMON. WHAT YOU WANT IS COLD-SMOKED SALMON WITH A MOIST BUT RELATIVELY NON-OILY CONSISTENCY AND A GOOD, SMOKY FLAVOUR.

THE FRENCH-STYLE, SLIGHTLY FERMENTED THICK CREAM KNOWN AS CRÈME FRAÎCHE GIVES THE POTATOES A LUSCIOUSLY RICH SAUCE AND THROWS THE QUALITIES OF THE SALMON INTO SHARP RELIEF JUST AS CREAM CHEESE DOES. IF YOU CANNOT FIND CRÈME FRAÎCHE, YOU COULD USE SOURED CREAM OR FROMAGE FRAIS. KEPT REFRIGERATED AS THEY SHOULD BE, THESE PRODUCTS TEND TO BECOME QUITE THICK; YOU MIGHT WANT TO TAKE OFF THE LID FIRST TO CHECK AND, IF THAT IS THE CASE WITH YOUR CREAM, LET IT STAND AT ROOM TEMPERATURE FOR A LITTLE WHILE TO LOOSEN UP BEFORE YOU MIX IT WITH THE POTATOES. IF YOU DON'T, THOUGH, DON'T WORRY TOO MUCH; THE WARMTH OF THE POTATOES WILL GRADUALLY MELT THE CREAM.

Prawn and Baby Vegetable Salad

SERVES 4

SALAD

350g (12oz) assorted baby vegetables
675g (1½lb) mixed baby salad leaves
350g (12oz) cooked peeled prawns
Fresh dill sprigs, for garnish

DRESSING

4 tablespoons lemon juice
½ teaspoon caster sugar
½ teaspoon salt
¼ teaspoon white pepper
1 tablespoon finely snipped fresh dill
125ml (4fl oz) extra virgin olive oil

1. At least 1 hour and up to several hours before serving the salad, use a steamer to steam the baby vegetables until tender but still crisp; this should take no more than 3 to 5 minutes. Alternatively, put the vegetables in a bowl, add a splash of water, cover with microwave cling film and microwave the vegetables on high until just tender, 1 to 2 minutes, depending on the wattage of your oven. When uncovering the vegetables, take care to lift the lid or film away from you to avoid being burned by the steam. Transfer the vegetables to a covered bowl and cool in the refrigerator.

2. Before serving the salad, make the dressing. In a small mixing bowl, stir together the lemon juice, sugar, salt, pepper and dill until the sugar and salt dissolve. Stirring continuously, slowly pour in the olive oil.

Spoon a little of the dressing over the baby vegetables, tossing gently to coat them lightly.

3. Put the salad leaves in a large mixing bowl, add the rest of the dressing and toss to coat the leaves.

4. Arrange the salad leaves on large, chilled individual serving plates. Arrange the baby vegetables and prawns on top. Garnish with dill sprigs and serve immediately.

TEST KITCHEN NOTES

EVERYONE LOVES BABY VEGETABLES AND BABY SALAD GREENS, SO THIS RECIPE WAS CREATED TO CELEBRATE THESE SUCCULENT MORSELS.

BABY COURGETTES, BABY CARROTS, DOLL-HOUSE-SIZE CAULIFLOWERS, AND BABY BEETROOTS AND SWEETCORN—ALL THESE AND MORE ARE AVAILABLE. SO, TOO, ARE ANY TINY BITES OF VEGETABLE YOU CAN CONSTRUCT FROM LARGER ONES YOU BUY, SUCH AS SMALL FLORETS OF BROCCOLI OR THE LITTLEST MANGETOUT OR SUGAR SNAP PEAS YOU CAN SELECT.

COOKED PEELED PRAWNS ARE THE PERFECT TOPPING. ADD A LEMON-DILL VINAIGRETTE AND YOU HAVE THE LIGHTEST MAIN MEAL SALAD IMAGINABLE.

Seared Fresh Tuna Salad with Wasabi Dressing

SERVES 4

DRESSING

1 tablespoon *wasabi* powder
½ tablespoon cold water
1 tablespoon *tamari*
1 tablespoon lemon juice

SALAD

2 tablespoons seasoned rice vinegar
2 tablespoons *tamari*
2 tablespoons toasted sesame oil
350g (12oz) fresh tuna fillet
4 small round lettuces, leaves separated
25g (1oz) pickled pink ginger
15g (½oz) fresh chives, finely chopped
25–55g (1–2oz) sesame seeds, toasted
    (see page 17)

1. First, make the dressing. In a small bowl, stir together the *wasabi* powder and water until they form a smooth paste. Stir in the *tamari* and lemon juice, cover and refrigerate.

2. To prepare the tuna, put the rice vinegar, *tamari* and sesame oil in a shallow bowl large enough to hold the fillet and stir them together. Add the tuna and turn to coat it with the marinade. Cover the bowl and refrigerate for 1 hour.

3. Before serving, sort through the lettuce leaves, selecting the best specimens, and arrange them on large, chilled individual serving plates.

4. Over medium-high heat, heat a small non-stick frying pan just large enough to hold the fillet. Put the tuna in the pan and sear it for 30 to 45 seconds per side.
    Remove the tuna from the pan. If it is wide, cut it in half lengthways. Cut it crossways into 5mm (¼in) thick slices.

5. Arrange the tuna slices on top of the lettuce leaves. Drizzle the dressing evenly over the tuna and garnish each piece with some pickled ginger, chives and sesame seeds. Serve immediately.

TEST KITCHEN NOTES

IF YOU'RE A LOVER OF SUSHI, THIS IS ABSOLUTELY THE MAIN MEAL SALAD FOR YOU. FINE RAW TUNA IS MARINATED HERE IN A MIXTURE OF SEASONED RICE VINEGAR, SOY SAUCE AND TOASTED SESAME OIL—ALL AVAILABLE IN JAPANESE FOOD SHOPS OR WELL-STOCKED SUPERMARKETS—AND THEN BRIEFLY SEARED ON ALL SIDES OVER HIGH HEAT TO SEAL IN THE FLAVOURINGS WITHOUT REALLY COOKING THE FISH. THEN THE TUNA IS CUT INTO BITE-SIZE SLICES AND ARRANGED ON TOP OF SMALL LETTUCE LEAVES, HIGHLIGHTING THE FISH'S BEAUTIFUL DEEP RED COLOUR. FINALLY, THE TUNA IS GARNISHED WITH PICKLED GINGER, CHIVES, SESAME SEEDS AND A DRESSING FLAVOURED WITH *WASABI*—A FIERY GREEN JAPANESE HORSERADISH POWDER FOUND, LIKE THE GINGER, IN JAPANESE DELIS.

BE SURE TO BUY YOUR TUNA FROM A RELIABLE FISHMONGER. THE FILLET SHOULD BE UNDENIABLY FRESH, FREE OF ANY 'OFF' AROMA.

Prawn-and-Pasta-Shell Pineapple Boats

SERVES 4

SALAD

2 medium-size ripe pineapples with
    leaves attached
175g (6oz) dried small pasta shells
350g (12oz) cooked peeled prawns
1 x 225g (8oz) can sliced water chest-
    nuts, drained
1 red pepper, quartered, seeded and cut
    into 5mm (¼in) dice
½ small red onion, finely chopped
1 teaspoon salt
1 teaspoon white pepper
Fresh mint sprigs, for garnish

DRESSING

175g (6oz) mayonnaise
2 tablespoons frozen orange juice
    concentrate, thawed
2 tablespoons lemon juice
2 tablespoons grated lemon zest
1 tablespoon finely chopped fresh
    coriander leaves
1 tablespoon finely chopped fresh
    mint leaves

1. Using a large, sharp knife, carefully cut the pineapples in half, cutting from their stalk ends evenly through the fruit and through their crowns of leaves (see Test Kitchen Notes). Using a small, sharp knife and carefully working in small sections at a time, cut out the fruit from each half, leaving a shell about 1cm (½in) thick. Cut out and discard the tough central core from the fruit you remove. Coarsely chop the fruit and transfer it to a large mixing bowl. Holding each pineapple half over the bowl, use your fingertips or a spoon to scrape the juice from some of the fruit that remains clinging to the shell, letting the juice drop into the bowl. Cover the bowl of fruit and the hollowed-out pineapple boats with cling film and refrigerate.

2. Bring a large saucepan of water to the boil. Add the pasta shells and cook until tender but still chewy, 8 to 10 minutes, or according to the packet directions. Drain the shells and rinse under cold running water to cool them, then drain well again.

3. Transfer the pasta shells to the bowl of chopped pineapple. Add the prawns, water chestnuts, pepper and onion. Sprinkle on the salt and white pepper and toss to mix.

4. Prepare the dressing. In a small mixing bowl, stir together the mayonnaise, orange juice concentrate, lemon juice and zest, coriander and mint. Pour this dressing over the pineapple mixture and toss well to coat the ingredients.

5. To serve the salads, place a pineapple boat on each large individual serving plate or bowl. With a large spoon, fill each boat with the salad, mounding the mixture generously above the rim of the boat. Garnish with mint sprigs and serve immediately.

TEST KITCHEN NOTES

THE CROWN OF SPIKY LEAVES LOOKS ESPECIALLY PRETTY WHEN YOU'VE CUT THE PINEAPPLES LENGTHWAYS IN HALF TO MAKE THE BOATS, SO DON'T CUT THE TOP OFF. CUTTING THE PINEAPPLE IS AN AWKWARD JOB. USE A LARGE, SHARP, SERRATED BREAD KNIFE AND WORK ON A NON-SLIP CUTTING BOARD. BE SURE ALWAYS TO CUT AWAY FROM YOURSELF AND TO KEEP YOUR FINGERS WELL CLEAR OF THE KNIFE WHILE YOU STEADY THE FRUIT. TAKE EQUAL CARE WHEN HOLLOWING OUT EACH PINEAPPLE HALF, CUTTING OUT THE FRUIT IN SECTIONS TO MAINTAIN THE SHAPE OF THE BOATS AND THE SAFETY OF YOUR HANDS.

Bravocado

SALAD

225g (8oz) mixed salad greens
2 large, ripe avocados
1 lemon, cut in half
2 navel oranges
350g (12oz) cooked crabmeat, picked
    over to remove all bits of shell and
    cartilage
350g (12oz) cooked peeled prawns
1 small red onion, cut into very thin slices
2 tablespoons finely chopped
    fresh flat-leaf parsley
2 tablespoons finely chopped
    fresh chives

DRESSING

Juice reserved from segmenting oranges
115g (4oz) mayonnaise
75g (6oz) bottled tomato-chilli sauce

1. To assemble the salad, arrange the greens in large, chilled, shallow individual serving bowls.

2. Cut each avocado in half and remove the stone. Rub the exposed surfaces of the avocado halves generously with the cut lemon, gently squeezing the lemon halves as you do. Nestle an avocado half in each bed of lettuce.

3. With a sharp knife, cut off the ends of the oranges in slices thick enough to reveal the fruit; reserve the slices. One at a time, stand the oranges on their navel ends and cut off the peel in strips thick enough to remove the membranes and reveal the fruit; reserve the peel. Holding each orange in your hand over a small mixing bowl, use a small, sharp knife to cut between the fruit and membrane of each segment, allowing it to drop into the bowl.

Remove the orange segments from the bowl and arrange them around the avocado halves. Take the reserved strips of peel and squeeze them gently over the bowl, one at a time, to extract the juice from the fruit that adheres to them. Set the bowl of juice aside.

4. In another bowl, toss together the crabmeat and prawns. Pile the seafood into the centre of each avocado half, allowing it to tumble over on to the bed of greens. Sprinkle the red onion on top.

5. Into the bowl of orange juice stir the mayonnaise and tomato-chilli sauce to make a creamy but liquid dressing. Drizzle the dressing all over each salad. Garnish with parsley and chives and serve immediately.

TEST KITCHEN NOTES

THIS DELICIOUS SALAD WILL ELICIT BRAVOS FROM EVEN THE MOST DISCRIMINATING OF DINNER GUESTS.

THIS RECIPE BEGINS WITH THE TYPICAL SEAFOOD-STUFFED AVOCADO, BUT THEN TAKES THE CONCEPT SEVERAL STEPS FURTHER BY ADDING THE SPARK OF RED ONION AND SWEET ORANGE SEGMENTS, THEN DRESSING THE ENTIRE SALAD WITH AN APPEALINGLY SWEET-TANGY BLEND OF TOMATO-CHILLI SAUCE, MAYONNAISE AND ORANGE JUICE.

THE SALAD GOES TOGETHER VERY QUICKLY, SINCE YOU'RE USING READY-PREPARED INGREDIENTS: COOKED CRABMEAT AND PRAWNS AND BOUGHT MAYONNAISE AND TOMATO-CHILLI SAUCE. THE MOST ARDUOUS WORK YOU HAVE TO DO IS CUT OUT THE ORANGE SEGMENTS, WHICH TAKES BUT A FEW MINUTES AND YIELDS THE JUICE THAT THINS AND SWEETENS THE DRESSING.

YOU COULD MAKE THE SALAD, IF YOU LIKE, ENTIRELY WITH CRAB OR PRAWNS. IF POSSIBLE, WHENEVER USING AVOCADO IN A SALAD, ALWAYS BUY THE DARK, BUMPY-SKINNED HASS VARIETY, WHICH WILL GIVE YOU THE BEST FLAVOUR AND TEXTURE.

Grilled Crab Cake Salad with Chinese Leaf and Lemon-Mustard-Cream Dressing

SERVES 4

DRESSING

4 tablespoons lemon juice

¾ teaspoon caster sugar

¼ teaspoon salt

¼ teaspoon white pepper

2 teaspoons grainy Dijon mustard

225ml (8fl oz) double cream

1 tablespoon finely chopped fresh basil

1 tablespoon finely chopped fresh chives

SALAD

350g (12oz) freshly cooked crabmeat, picked over to remove pieces of shell and cartilage

2 large eggs, lightly beaten

55g (2oz) fine, fresh white breadcrumbs

115g (4oz) mayonnaise

6 tablespoons whipping cream

3 tablespoons finely chopped fresh chives

3 tablespoons finely chopped fresh flat-leaf parsley

1 large ripe avocado

1 tablespoon lemon juice

1 head Chinese leaf

2 red peppers, roasted, peeled and seeded (see pages 15–16), then cut into strips

12 sprigs fresh watercress, for garnish

1 lemon, cut into 8 wedges, for garnish

1. First, make the dressing. In a mixing bowl, use a wire whisk to stir together the lemon juice, sugar, salt and pepper until the sugar and salt dissolve. Add the mustard and stir until blended. Whisking continuously, slowly pour in the cream, continuing to whisk until the mixture is thick but still fluid. Stir in the herbs. Cover the bowl and refrigerate.

2. To make the crab cake mixture, put the crabmeat, eggs, breadcrumbs, mayonnaise, cream, chives and parsley in a mixing bowl. With your hands, mix them together until well blended. Cover with cling film and refrigerate until chilled, at least 1 hour.

3. Preheat the grill. Line a baking sheet large enough to hold all the crab cakes with foil. Spray the foil with non-stick cooking spray or brush with oil.

4. Halve the avocado and remove the stone. Cut each half lengthways into 6 thin wedges and remove the peel from each. Put the lemon juice in a shallow bowl and gently turn the avocado wedges in it to coat them.

5. Using a 5cm (2in) pastry cutter or tumbler, form 12 crab cakes about 5cm (2in) in diameter and 2.5cm (1in) thick, placing them on the foil-lined sheet.

6. Cut the Chinese leaves crossways into strips about 1cm (½in) wide. Discard the cores. Put the strips in a mixing bowl, add the dressing and toss well to coat. Arrange the Chinese leaf on large, chilled individual serving plates.

7. Grill the crab cakes until golden brown, about 3 minutes per side. Place 3 crab cakes on each bed of Chinese leaf. Garnish each plate with avocado slices, roasted pepper strips and watercress sprigs. Place 2 wedges of lemon on each plate to be squeezed over the crab cakes to taste. Serve immediately.

> ### TEST KITCHEN NOTES
>
> BUY THE BEST COOKED CRABMEAT YOU CAN FIND, AND FRESH RATHER THAN FROZEN OR CANNED. YOU CAN ALSO, OF COURSE, BUY A COOKED CRAB AND EXTRACT THE MEAT YOURSELF.

Classic Seafood Salad

DRESSING

115g (4 oz) mayonnaise

175ml (6fl oz) bottled tomato-chilli sauce

2 tablespoons lemon juice

SALAD

675g (1½lb) cos lettuce leaves, torn into
bite-size pieces

1 large, ripe avocado

1 tablespoon lemon juice

350g (12oz) cooked crabmeat, picked
over to remove all bits of shell and
cartilage

350g (12oz) cooked peeled prawns

3 plum tomatoes, cored and cut into
quarters

3 large eggs, hard-boiled, shelled and
cut into quarters

Flat-leaf parsley sprigs, for garnish

1. First, make the dressing. Put the mayonnaise, tomato-chilli sauce and lemon juice in a small mixing bowl and stir well until blended. Set aside.

2. Arrange the lettuce in beds on large, chilled individual serving plates or bowls.

3. Halve the avocado and remove the stone. Cut each half lengthways into 6 thin wedges and remove the peel from each. Put the lemon juice in a shallow bowl and gently turn the avocado wedges in it to coat them.

4. Arrange the crabmeat and prawns on top of each bed of lettuce. Place 3 avocado wedges, 3 tomato wedges and 3 wedges of egg on each plate. Drizzle the dressing over each serving, garnish with parsley and serve immediately.

TEST KITCHEN NOTES

THIS IS THE SORT OF MAIN MEAL SALAD YOU MIGHT FIND ON THE MENU OF A SEASIDE HOTEL RESTAURANT. NOTHING IN THE RECIPE IS OUT OF THE ORDINARY; EVERY INGREDIENT IS REASSURINGLY FAMILIAR.

OF COURSE, YOU COULD MAKE THIS SALAD ENTIRELY WITH CRAB ALONE OR WITH JUST PRAWNS; AND IF FRESHLY COOKED LOBSTER MEAT OR OTHER SHELLFISH LIKE SCALLOPS OR LANGOUSTINES ARE AVAILABLE AT A REASONABLE PRICE, DON'T HESITATE TO SUBSTITUTE THEM.

SERVE THIS SALAD WITH HOT CRUSTY BREAD.

Vietnamese Prawn and Rice Stick Salad

SERVES 4

DRESSING

175ml (6fl oz) seasoned rice vinegar
6 tablespoons finely chopped pickled
    pink ginger
3 fresh green chillies
1 tablespoon toasted sesame oil

SALAD

350g (12oz) rice stick noodles
1 head Chinese leaf
2 carrots
½ cucumber
350g (12oz) cooked peeled prawns
15g (½oz) fresh mint leaves, finely
    chopped
15g (½oz) fresh basil leaves, finely
    shredded
55g (2oz) dry-roasted peanuts

1. First, make the dressing. Put the rice vinegar in a small mixing bowl and stir in the ginger. Halve the chillies (make sure to wash your hands thoroughly after handling chillies, avoiding contact with the sensitive skin around your eyes, nose and mouth before you do). If you want a hotter dressing, leave the seeds in; if not, remove them. Finely chop the chillies and add them to the bowl. Stir in the sesame oil and set the

dressing aside.

2. To make the salad, first prepare the rice sticks. Bring a kettle of water to the boil. Meanwhile, put the rice sticks in a large sieve and rinse well with cold running water. Transfer them to a large bowl. Pour boiling water over them until they are submerged. Leave them to soak for 1 minute, then drain in the sieve and rinse with cold running water to cool them. Drain again.

3. With a large knife, cut the head of Chinese leaf crossways into thin shreds, discarding the cores. Arrange the shreds on large individual serving plates.

4. Using the fine side of a grater, grate the carrots lengthways into thin shreds. Arrange the carrot shreds on top of the shreds of Chinese leaf, leaving a ring of Chinese leaf showing.

5. Arrange the rice sticks in a bed on top of the carrots, leaving a ring of carrots showing.

6. Using the larger side of the grater, grate the cucumber lengthways into thicker shreds. Arrange the cucumber shreds to form nests on top of the rice sticks, leaving a ring of rice sticks showing.

7. Place the prawns on top of the nest of cucumber shreds.

8. Spoon the dressing evenly all over the salads. Garnish with the mint and basil and scatter the peanuts on top. Serve immediately.

TEST KITCHEN NOTES

YOU CAN FIND THE INGREDIENTS FOR THIS SALAD WITHOUT TOO MUCH TROUBLE. MANY SUPERMARKETS SELL RICE STICK NOODLES, SEASONED RICE VINEGAR AND TOASTED SESAME OIL IN THEIR ORIENTAL FOODS SECTIONS; IF NOT, SEEK OUT A JAPANESE FOOD SHOP AND YOU'LL FIND THEM THERE, ALONG WITH PICKLED PINK GINGER SLICES, IN JARS OR FRESH AND REFRIGERATED. AS FOR THOSE RICE STICKS, YOU MAY ALSO FIND THEM UNDER THE CHINESE NAME *MAI FUN* OR CALLED RICE VERMICELLI. THEY LOOK LIKE THINLY SPUN THREADS, AS FINE AS ANGEL HAIR PASTA. MADE FROM ALREADY COOKED RICE, THEY REQUIRE JUST A BRIEF SOFTENING WITH BOILING WATER.

Grilled Scallop and Sweet Onion Salad

SERVES 4

DRESSING

4 tablespoons balsamic vinegar
½ teaspoon salt
¼ teaspoon black pepper
175ml (6fl oz) extra virgin olive oil

SALAD

2 tablespoons lemon juice
4 tablespoons extra virgin olive oil
350g (12oz) scallops, trimmed of any
    tough white connective tissue
1 large sweet onion
Salt
White pepper
675g (1½lb) mixed baby salad leaves
175g (6oz) yellow or red baby plum or
    cherry tomatoes
25g (1oz) pine nuts, toasted (see
    page 17)
3 tablespoons finely shredded fresh
    basil leaves

1. First, make the dressing. In a small mixing bowl, with a fork or small wire whisk stir together the balsamic vinegar, salt and black pepper until the salt dissolves. Stirring continuously, add the olive oil in a thin, steady stream. Set aside.

2. To prepare the salad, stir together in a small bowl the lemon juice and half the olive oil. Then add the scallops, turning to coat them. Leave them to marinate at room temperature while you preheat the grill or barbecue.

3. Slice off the stalk and root ends of the onion. Cut the onion crossways into slices 5mm–1cm (¼–½in) thick. Brush the slices on both sides with the remaining olive oil.

4. Sprinkle the scallops and onion slices to taste with salt and white pepper, and grill or barbecue them until they are lightly golden brown, 2 to 3 minutes per side.

5. Meanwhile, put the salad leaves and tomatoes in a large mixing bowl and toss with enough dressing to coat them well. Arrange the leaves and tomatoes in attractive beds on large individual serving plates.

6. Separate the grilled onion slices into rings and place them over the salads (a fork may help you do this, as they will be hot). With a sharp knife, cut each scallop horizontally into two thinner rounds. Arrange the scallop halves golden sides up on top of the salads. Scatter the pine nuts on top and sprinkle with fresh basil shreds. Serve immediately.

TEST KITCHEN NOTES

I OWE THE INSPIRATION FOR THIS SALAD TO MICHAEL MCCARTY, OWNER OF THE ACCLAIMED MICHAEL'S RESTAURANTS IN SANTA MONICA, CALIFORNIA, AND NEW YORK CITY.

THIS VERSION FEATURES THE EYE-OPENING FLAVOUR COMBINATIONS OF MICHAEL'S SEAFOOD SALADS, BUT SIMPLIFIES THE PROCEDURE AND CHANGES SOME OF THE MORE ELABORATE RESTAURANT INGREDIENTS AND PRESENTATION STYLE. YOU COULD SUBSTITUTE SLICED PLUM TOMATOES FOR THE BABY PLUM OR CHERRY TOMATOES I CALL FOR. RED ONION COULD BE USED INSTEAD OF THE SWEET WHITE ONION. YOU COULD USE RAW KING OR TIGER PRAWNS INSTEAD OF THE SCALLOPS, ALTHOUGH THE MILKY SWEETNESS AND TENDER TEXTURE OF THE LATTER GO SO VERY WELL WITH THE GRILLED ONIONS AND SHARP-TASTING PINE NUTS.

Grilled Chicken and Orange Salad on Baby Spinach

SERVES 4

4 navel oranges, or other sweet, juicy
    oranges
¾ teaspoon salt
¾ teaspoon black pepper
225ml (8fl oz) extra virgin olive oil
4 boneless, skinless chicken breasts,
    115–175g (4–6oz) each
350g (12oz) baby spinach leaves,
    thoroughly washed
½ small red onion, very thinly sliced

1. With a sharp knife, cut a slice off each end of the oranges thick enough to expose the fruit beneath its outer membrane; set the slices aside. Stand each orange on a sliced end and, cutting from top to bottom, slice off the remainder of the peel in strips thick enough to remove all the white pith and outer membrane, revealing the fruit; reserve the strips of peel. Cut each orange crossways into slices about 1cm (½in) thick; set the larger slices aside, reserving the smaller top and bottom slices of fruit along with the pieces of peel.

2. Over a mixing bowl, use your hands to tightly squeeze the top and bottom slices of fruit to extract their juice. Likewise, squeeze the pieces of orange peel to extract juice from any fruit pulp adhering to their insides. Discard the peels.

3. Add the salt and pepper to the orange juice and stir with a fork or wire whisk until the salt dissolves. Stirring continuously, slowly pour in the olive oil.

4. Pour half of the resulting dressing into another mixing bowl. Add the chicken breasts and turn to coat them well. Leave to marinate for about 15 minutes.

5. Meanwhile, preheat the grill or barbecue.

6. Remove the chicken breasts from the marinade and discard the marinade. Season the chicken breasts with salt and pepper to taste. Grill or barbecue the chicken breasts until done, about 5 minutes per side. When you turn the chicken over to cook on the second side, dip the orange slices in the reserved dressing and cook them alongside the chicken until golden, 2 to 3 minutes per side.

7. Toss the spinach leaves with the remaining dressing and arrange them on large, chilled individual serving plates. Cut each chicken breast crossways into 1cm (½in) wide slices and arrange them and the orange slices on top of the spinach. Top each salad with red onion and serve immediately.

TEST KITCHEN NOTES

AS LIGHT ON THE PALATE AS IT IS ON THE STOMACH, THIS SALAD IS THE IDEAL MAIN COURSE FOR A SPECIAL OCCASION, WARM-WEATHER LUNCH. THE FLAVOURS ARE SPRIGHTLY, YET COMPLEX AND SATISFYING. THE ARRAY OF BRIGHT COLOURS AND PLEASING SHAPES JUST COULDN'T BE PRETTIER. DEPENDING UPON YOUR PREFERENCE AND THE STYLE OF THE OCCASION, YOU CAN PRESENT THE SALADS WITH THEIR INGREDIENTS NEATLY ARRANGED ON TOP OF THE SPINACH, AS THE INSTRUCTIONS HERE CALL FOR, OR ALL TOSSED TOGETHER.

Lemon Chicken and Pasta Salad

SERVES 4

DRESSING

4 tablespoons lemon juice

½ teaspoon caster sugar

½ teaspoon salt

¼ teaspoon white pepper

1 tablespoon Dijon mustard

1 tablespoon finely chopped fresh flat-
leaf parsley

1 tablespoon finely snipped fresh dill

1 tablespoon finely shredded fresh basil
leaves

175ml (6fl oz) extra virgin olive oil

SALAD

450g (1lb) boneless, skinless chicken
breasts

2 tablespoons lemon juice

1 tablespoon grated lemon zest

1 teaspoon caster sugar

2 tablespoons olive oil

350g (12oz) dried rainbow fusilli

24 large pitted black olives, broken
in half

2 red peppers roasted, peeled and seeded (see pages 15-16), then cut into
thin strips

½ small red onion, cut into very thin slices

350g (12oz) mixed salad leaves

25g (1oz) pine nuts, toasted (see
page 17)

1. Prepare the dressing. In a small bowl, stir together with a fork or small wire whisk the lemon juice, sugar, salt and pepper until the sugar and salt dissolve. Stir in the mustard until blended, then stir in the parsley, dill and basil. Stirring continuously, slowly pour in the olive oil. Set the dressing aside.

2. To make the salad, first marinate the chicken breasts. In a shallow dish large enough to hold the chicken in a single layer, stir together the lemon juice and zest and the sugar until the sugar dissolves; then stir in the olive oil. Add the chicken breasts and turn to coat them. Leave them to marinate for 15 to 30 minutes.

3. Meanwhile, preheat the grill or barbecue.

4. At the same time, bring a large pan of water to the boil over medium-high heat. Add the pasta and cook until tender but still chewy, 7 to 9 minutes or according to the packet instructions.

Drain the pasta in a sieve, rinse under cold running water until it is cool and drain well again. Transfer the pasta to a large mixing bowl, add 2 tablespoons of the dressing and toss well.

5. When the chicken is done, cut each breast lengthways in half again; then cut these strips crossways into 1cm (½in) wide pieces. Add them to the bowl of pasta and also add the black olives, roasted pepper strips, onion and remaining dressing. Toss well to coat all the ingredients. If not serving the salad immediately, cover the bowl with cling film and refrigerate.

6. To serve, arrange the salad leaves on large, chilled individual serving plates or shallow bowls. Mound the pasta salad on top and garnish with pine nuts.

> **TEST KITCHEN NOTES**
>
> I THINK OF THIS AS THE QUINTESSENTIAL MAIN MEAL PASTA SALAD FOR MANY REASONS. IT IS FILLING, AS ALL GOOD PASTA SALADS SHOULD BY NATURE BE, YET IT IS LIGHT AND REFRESHING IN ITS FLAVOURS, A PERFECT DISH TO SERVE WHEN THE WEATHER IS WARM OR WHEN YOU WISH IT WAS.

Japanese Chicken Salad

SERVES 4

CHICKEN

400ml (14fl oz) chicken stock

1 tablespoon soy sauce

4 thin slices fresh root ginger

350g (12oz) chicken breast strips

SALAD

4 tablespoons rice vinegar

1 teaspoon caster sugar

1 teaspoon salt

1 cucumber, cut crossways into very thin
    slices

350g (12oz) Japanese *soba* noodles

1 tablespoon toasted sesame oil

1 teaspoon soy sauce

1 small carrot, finely grated

1 spring onion, thinly sliced

2 teaspoons sesame seeds, toasted
    (see page 17)

1. Prepare the chicken at least 2 hours and up to 24 hours before serving time. Put the chicken stock, soy sauce and ginger slices in a medium saucepan and bring to the boil over medium-high heat. Reduce the heat to very low, add the chicken strips, cover and poach until cooked through, about 10 minutes. Let the chicken cool in the stock at room temperature for about 30 minutes, then transfer the chicken and stock to a bowl, cover with cling film and refrigerate until cold.

2. At least 30 minutes before serving time, prepare the cucumbers. Put the rice vinegar in a mixing bowl and stir in the sugar and salt until dissolved. Add the cucumber slices and toss well. Cover with cling film and refrigerate until serving time.

3. To assemble the salad, bring a large saucepan of water to the boil over medium-high heat. Add the *soba* noodles and boil until tender but still slightly chewy, about 5 minutes or according to the packet directions. Drain well in a colander, then rinse under cold running water until cool and drain well again. Transfer the noodles to a bowl and stir in the sesame oil and soy sauce.

4. Arrange the noodles on four large individual serving plates. Distribute the cucumber salad on top of the noodles. Remove the chicken strips from the stock, reserving the stock for another use, if you wish. Cut the chicken crossways into 1cm (½in) pieces and arrange them on top of the cucumbers. Garnish with grated carrot, spring onion and sesame seeds and serve immediately.

TEST KITCHEN NOTES

AS EXOTIC AS THIS SALAD MAY SEEM, ALL ITS INGREDIENTS CAN BE USUALLY FOUND IN A WELL-STOCKED SUPERMARKET.

THE BED OF DARK BROWN BUCKWHEAT SOBA NOODLES LENDS A PLEASINGLY EARTHY BASE TO A REFRESHING AND LIGHT-TASTING MIXTURE OF CRISP CUCUMBERS, POACHED CHICKEN AND HINTS OF RICE VINEGAR, SOY SAUCE AND SESAME.

FOR THE CHICKEN, I LIKE TO USE LONG, THIN STRIPS OF WHITE BREAST MEAT. IF USING WHOLE BONELESS, SKINLESS BREASTS INSTEAD, INCREASE THE POACHING TIME BY ABOUT 5 MINUTES AND, AFTER COOKING, CUT THE BREASTS IN HALF LENGTHWAYS BEFORE CUTTING CROSSWAYS INTO CHUNKS.

THIS SALAD PRESENTATION ALSO WORKS VERY WELL WITH RAW KING OR TIGER PRAWNS. PEEL AND DEVEIN THEM, LEAVING THE TAILS INTACT, AND POACH THEM FOR ABOUT HALF THE TIME REQUIRED FOR THE CHICKEN.

Grilled Duck Sausage Salad with Fresh Pear and Berry Vinaigrette

SERVES 4

DRESSING

6 tablespoons raspberry vinegar

½ teaspoon salt

¼ teaspoon white pepper

125ml (4fl oz) extra virgin olive oil

SALAD

4 fresh duck sausages or breasts (see test kitchen notes), about 115g (4oz) each

1 medium red onion, cut into 5mm–1cm (¼–½in) thick slices

2 tablespoons extra virgin olive oil

Salt

White pepper

350g (12oz) rocket leaves

350g (12oz) radicchio leaves, torn into bite-size pieces

2 large firm but ripe pears

175g (6oz) fresh, or frozen and thawed, raspberries

25g (21oz) pine nuts, toasted (see page 17)

15g (½oz) fresh basil leaves, finely shredded

1. Prepare the dressing. In a small bowl, stir together the raspberry vinegar, salt and white pepper until the salt dissolves. Stirring continuously, pour in the oil in a thin, steady stream. Set the dressing aside.

2. Preheat the grill or barbecue.

3. Put the sausages in a medium saucepan and add cold water to cover them. Over medium-high heat, bring the water to the boil. Drain the sausages immediately and prick each one in several places with the prongs of a fork.

4. Brush the onion slices on both sides with olive oil and season lightly with salt and white pepper.

5. Grill or barbecue the sausage and onions until they are evenly browned, 4 to 5 minutes per side.

6. While the sausage and onions are cooking, put the rocket and radicchio leaves in a bowl and toss them with about two thirds of the dressing. Arrange the leaves on large individual serving plates.

7. With a small, sharp knife, quarter the pears lengthways and cut out their cores and stalks. Cut each quarter lengthways into thin slices and arrange them on top of half of each salad.

8. With a fork, separate the onion rings and arrange them on top of the salad halves not covered by the pears. Cut each sausage diagonally into 1cm (½in) slices and arrange them on top of the onion rings. Scatter the raspberries all over each salad and garnish with the pine nuts and shredded basil. Serve immediately.

TEST KITCHEN NOTES

HERE IS A FINE EXAMPLE OF HOW A RICH AND SATISFYING MAIN INGREDIENT CAN BE TRANSFORMED INTO A LIGHT SALAD. THE SECRET, IN THIS CASE, LIES IN SELECTING ACCOMPANYING INGREDIENTS—IN THIS CASE, FRESH FRUIT AND A BERRY-SCENTED DRESSING—THAT OFFER SHARP, BRIGHT CONTRAST TO ITS RICHNESS, YIELDING AN OVERALL REFRESHING EFFECT THAT ALLOWS ONE TO LEAVE THE TABLE FEELING SATISFIED BUT NOT OVERFULL.

YOU CAN ALWAYS MAKE THIS SALAD WITH BONELESS DUCK BREASTS, USING ONE BREAST PER SERVING. MAKE A LITTLE EXTRA RASPBERRY VINAIGRETTE, PUT IT IN A SEPARATE BOWL AND MARINATE THE DUCK BREASTS IN IT FOR ABOUT 30 MINUTES. THEN SEASON WITH SALT AND PEPPER AND GRILL OR BARBECUE UNTIL THEY ARE DONE TO YOUR LIKING: FOR MEDIUM-RARE, 3 TO 4 MINUTES PER SIDE.

Shaved Fennel Salad with Parma Ham and Parmesan

SERVES 4

DRESSING

4 tablespoons lemon juice
½ teaspoon salt
½ teaspoon caster sugar
¼ teaspoon white pepper
175ml (6fl oz) extra virgin olive oil

SALAD

4 fennel bulbs, about 1.3kg (3lb) total
175g (6oz) Parma ham, very thinly sliced
115g (4oz), or more, piece Parmesan
   cheese
15g (½oz) fresh basil leaves, finely
   shredded

1. To make the dressing, stir together in a small bowl the lemon juice, salt, sugar and pepper until the salt and sugar dissolve. Stirring continuously, slowly pour in the olive oil. Set the dressing aside.

2. With a sharp knife, trim off the stalk and root ends of the fennel bulbs. Cut each bulb in half, top to bottom. Place each half cut side down and cut it crossways as thinly as possible to make thin strips. Put the fennel strips in a mixing bowl and toss with enough of the dressing to coat well.

3. Arrange the fennel salad on large, chilled individual serving plates. Drape the slices of Parma ham on top of the fennel. Hold the piece of Parmesan over each salad and, with a cheese shaver or a swivel-blade vegetable peeler, cut the cheese into wide, thin shavings, letting them fall on top of the ham and using about 15g (½oz) of cheese per salad. Garnish each serving with shredded basil.

TEST KITCHEN NOTES

THIS SALAD REMINDS ME OF A SUNNY AFTERNOON ON A *TERRAZZO* IN ITALY. IT IS INSPIRED, IN FACT, BY THE KIND OF FENNEL SALAD YOU MIGHT WELL FIND ON AN ITALIAN ANTIPASTO TABLE: THIN STRIPS OF THE CRISP, LIQUORICE-SCENTED BULB DRESSED WITH A SIMPLE LEMON VINAIGRETTE AND TOPPED WITH PARMESAN SHAVINGS. IN THIS CASE, IT WAS MY OWN IDEA TO ADD *PROSCIUTTO DI PARMA*, THE FAMED DRIED RAW HAM, WHICH YOU CAN FIND IN ANY WELL-STOCKED SUPERMARKET OR DELICATESSEN. NO DOUBT, YOU'D FIND SUCH A CREATION SOMEWHERE ON A TOUR OF TUSCANY.

BEFITTING THE SPIRIT OF THE SALAD, I SUGGEST SERVING IT AS A WARM-WEATHER LUNCH, ACCOMPANIED SIMPLY BY A CRUSTY LOAF OF GOOD, PEASANT-STYLE BREAD, SOME SOFTENED UNSALTED BUTTER FOR SPREADING AND A CRISP, COOL ITALIAN WHITE WINE SUCH AS A VERDICCHIO OR PINOT GRIGIO.

Parma Ham and Minted Melon Salad

SERVES 4

1 honeydew melon
1 charentais or ogen melon
4 tablespoons lemon juice
85g (3oz) honey
3 tablespoons finely chopped fresh
    mint leaves
175g (6oz) Parma ham, very thinly sliced
225g (8oz) mixed baby salad leaves
85g (3oz) feta cheese, crumbled
    (optional)
Fresh mint sprigs, for garnish

1. Halve and seed the melons. If you like, use a melon ball scoop to remove the flesh in neat balls, transferring them to a mixing bowl. Alternatively, peel the rind from each melon half and cut the flesh into slices or neat chunks approximately 2.5cm (1in) across.

2. Drizzle the lemon juice and honey over the melon pieces and toss well to coat them. Sprinkle on the chopped mint and toss again. If not serving the salad immediately, cover the bowl with cling film and refrigerate for up to several hours.

3. Divide the melon pieces equally among four large, shallow, chilled serving bowls. Neatly drape the slices of Parma ham on top of the melon. Then arrange the baby salad leaves in beds next to the ham. Garnish with crumbled feta cheese, if using. Garnish each serving with a mint sprig.

Steak and Pasta Salad with Cherry Tomatoes

SERVES 4

DRESSING

225ml (8fl oz) Ranch Dressing (see page 26)

SALAD

350g (12oz) dried wheel-shaped pasta
24 cherry tomatoes, cut in half
½ teaspoon salt
450g (1lb) cooked steak, cooled and cut into thin, bite-size pieces
½ small red onion, thinly sliced
85g (3oz) rocket, stalks removed
350g (12oz) mixed baby salad greens
2 tablespoons coarsely chopped fresh flat-leaf parsley

1. Prepare the dressing and set it aside.

2. Bring a large saucepan of water to the boil over medium-high heat. Add the pasta and cook until tender but still chewy, about 8 minutes or according to the packet directions.

3. Drain the pasta in a colander and rinse under cold running water until the pasta is cool. Drain well.

4. In a small mixing bowl, toss together the cherry tomato halves and the salt.

5. Put the pasta in a mixing bowl and add the tomatoes, steak, onion and rocket. Toss gently to mix. Add the dressing and toss again until all the ingredients are evenly coated.

6. Arrange the baby salad leaves on large, chilled individual serving plates or bowls. Mound the salad on top and garnish with parsley.

TEST KITCHEN NOTES

THIS IS A GREAT RECIPE TO USE WHEN YOU HAVE GRILLED OR BARBECUED STEAK THE NIGHT BEFORE AND HAVE SOME LEFT OVER. IT ALSO WORKS WELL WITH LEFT-OVER ROAST BEEF. IF YOU WANT TO COOK SOME STEAK ESPECIALLY FOR IT, JUST RUB THE MEAT WITH A LITTLE OLIVE OIL AND SPRINKLE GENEROUSLY WITH SALT AND PEPPER, THEN COOK TO TASTE; BE SURE TO ALLOW TIME FOR THE MEAT TO COOL BEFORE ASSEMBLING THE SALAD.

NOTE THAT IN THE RECIPE INSTRUCTIONS I CALL FOR THE CHERRY TOMATOES TO BE LIGHTLY SALTED BEFORE YOU ADD THEM TO THE OTHER INGREDIENTS. IN THIS PARTICULAR CONTEXT, WITH THE TOMATOES SET AGAINST THE PASTA AND CREAMY DRESSING, I FOUND THIS PRELIMINARY SALTING PUT THEIR FLAVOUR INTO SHARPER RELIEF. BUT IF YOU'RE TRYING TO CUT BACK ON SALT, YOU CAN OMIT THIS STEP.

THE ROCKET LEAVES ADD A PLEASING DASH OF DARK GREEN COLOUR AND A HINT OF BITTERNESS TO THE MIXTURE. IF ROCKET IS UNAVAILABLE, SUBSTITUTE BABY SPINACH LEAVES.

IF YOU PREFER, YOU COULD USE CLASSIC BLUE CHEESE DRESSING (SEE PAGE 25) OR A SIMPLE VINAIGRETTE OF BALSAMIC VINEGAR, DIJON MUSTARD AND OLIVE OIL IN PLACE OF THE RANCH DRESSING.

Tropical Fruit Sunburst

SERVES 4

DRESSING

175g (6oz) honey, at room temperature
4 tablespoons lime juice
½ teaspoon chilli powder

SALAD

2 ripe pineapples, well chilled
2 ripe mangoes, well chilled
2 ripe paw paws, well chilled
4 ripe bananas
Fresh mint sprigs, for garnish

1. To make the dressing, stir together the honey and lime juice in a small mixing bowl until blended. Stir in the chilli powder and set aside.

2. To prepare the salad, first peel the pineapples. With a large, sharp knife, cut off the top and bottom of a pineapple. Stand the pineapple upright and, slicing downwards, peel away its skin in thick strips. With the tip of a small, sharp knife, cut out any remaining tough 'eyes' from the fruit. With the pineapple still upright, cut downwards to slice the fruit away from the thick, woody central core; discard the core. Cut the fruit into long spears.

3. With a small, sharp knife, peel the mangoes. Then cut the fruit away from the large, flat central stones in thick slices. Cut the slices into long strips. Set aside with the pineapple.

4. Halve, peel and seed the paw paws and cut them lengthways into 1cm (½in) thick slices. Set them aside with the mango and pineapple.

5. Finally, peel the bananas and cut them lengthways into halves or thirds.

6. Arrange the fruit in a starburst pattern on large, chilled individual serving plates. With a spoon, drizzle the dressing evenly all over the fruit. Garnish with mint sprigs and serve immediately.

TEST KITCHEN NOTES

NOTHING CAN QUITE PREPARE YOU FOR HOW STARTLINGLY GOOD THIS SALAD TASTES. THE SECRET LIES IN THE HINT OF CHILLI POWDER THAT SPICES UP THE HONEY AND LIME JUICE IN THE SALAD'S DRESSING. IT MAY SEEM ODD, I KNOW. THE CONCEPT RAISED MY EYEBROWS WHEN A CHEF FIRST SERVED ME HIS CHOCOLATE CHILLI ICE CREAM. I WAS DELIGHTED, THOUGH, BY THE WAY THE WHISPER OF CHILLI DEEPENED THE CHOCOLATE'S RICH FLAVOUR AND THEN LEFT JUST A SUSPICION OF AFTER-BURN ON THE PALATE.

THE CHILLI SERVES A SIMILAR ROLE HERE. YOU MIGHT NOT EVEN KNOW IT IS THERE ON FIRST TASTE, THOUGH YOU WILL SEE BRICK RED SPECKS DOTTING THE FRUIT. ALL YOU'LL SENSE IS THAT THE FRUIT TASTES SOMEHOW SWEETER, THE CITRUSY HONEY MORE EXOTIC. THEN, JUST AS THE COOL FLAVOURS HAVE PASSED, YOU'LL WONDER WHY YOU FEEL A LITTLE BIT OF HEAT IN YOUR MOUTH. AND JUST AS, SAY, THE SALT OF PEANUTS MAKES YOU WANT TO DRINK MORE BEER, SO TOO DOES THE WARMTH OF THE CHILLI SEND YOU BACK FOR ANOTHER TASTE OF THE FRUIT. IN SHORT, IT'S THE PERFECT SALAD FOR LUNCH ON A SULTRY DAY.

Summer Fruit Platter with Fresh Berry Yogurt

SERVES 4

FRESH BERRY YOGURT DIP

450g (1lb) very ripe fresh berries

3 tablespoons honey

Grated zest of 1 lemon

700ml (1¼ pints) plain yogurt

SALAD

1 charentais melon

4 plums

2 peaches

2 nectarines

450g (1lb) cherries, whole with stalks or
  stoned and stalks removed.

Fresh mint sprigs, for garnish

1. Begin by making the dip. First sort through the berries, removing any stalks and reserving several attractive berries for decorating. Put the remaining berries in a mixing bowl and, using a potato masher or a fork, begin to mash them up. As soon as some of their juices show, drizzle in the honey and sprinkle in the lemon zest. Continue mashing until the berries are coarsely puréed, with some small lumps still showing. Stir in the yogurt until well blended, then cover with cling film and refrigerate.

2. Shortly before serving time, prepare the fruit. Cut the melon into thin wedges, scoop out the seeds and, with a sharp knife, carefully cut away the peel. Halve and stone the plums, peaches and nectarines and cut them into wedges.

3. Divide the yogurt among four small bowls, each one in the centre of a large, chilled serving plate. Arrange the fruit wedges round the bowl and intersperse the cherries, stalks on. Decorate the yogurt with the reserved whole berries and sprigs of mint. Alternately, arrange all the fruit on the chilled plates, decorate with mint and serve the yogurt on the side as a dressing. Serve immediately.

TEST KITCHEN NOTES

THE BEST ADVICE I CAN GIVE YOU ON THIS SALAD IS THAT IT SHOULD BE DIFFERENT EVERY SINGLE TIME YOU MAKE IT, REFLECTING THE EVER-CHANGING ARRAY OF WONDERFUL SUMMER FRUITS AVAILABLE IN THE BEST LOCAL GREENGROCER'S MARKET OR SUPERMARKET YOU CAN FIND.

MELONS ARE A MUST, WHETHER CHARENTAIS, HONEYDEW, OGEN, GALIA OR ANY OF THE OTHER LUSCIOUS VARIETIES. (WATERMELON, HOWEVER, IS A LESS LIKELY CANDIDATE BECAUSE IT DOESN'T REALLY GO AS WELL WITH THE YOGURT DIP.) BUT THE REAL STARS OF THIS SALAD SHOULD BE JUICY SUMMER STONE FRUIT: PEACHES, OF COURSE, AND PREFERABLY A FREESTONE VARIETY. NECTARINES, NATURALLY. PLUMS CAN ADD GREAT VARIETY; I'M ESPECIALLY PARTIAL TO THE DEEP GARNET-COLOURED FRIAR ONES, AS WELL AS THE REDDISH-ORANGE SANTA ROSA PLUMS. CHERRIES ADD A FINAL, FESTIVE NOTE, WHETHER THE MOST COMMON DARK RED ONES OR, MY FAVOURITES, THE BLUSHING YELLOW-RED CHERRIES.

Suppliers

All the recipes in this book use ingredients that are widely available. When ingredients are called for that might be a bit specialised, the recipe's Test Kitchen Notes suggest where you can find them or what you can use in their place.

If you cannot find particular ingredients, or if you like to seek out new products through the mail, please refer to the following list of suppliers for salad-related products, including not only ingredients but also cookware. Write, phone or fax for further information.

GENERAL SPECIALIST INGREDIENTS

Chatsworth Farm Shop
Stud Farm
Pilsley
Bakewell
Derbyshire DE45 1UF
Tel: 01246 583392
Fax: 01246 583464
Mail order and retail; breads, cheeses and sausages, as well as local produce and products

L'Emporium
151 Draycott Avenue
London SW3 3AL
Tel: 0171 460 6100
Fax: 0171 460 6101
Retail; international range of cheese, oils, vinegars, condiments, fresh produce and breads

Fine Food Club
Unit 43, Vanalloys Business Park
Busgrove Lane
Oxfordshire RG9 5QB
Tel: 01491 682311
Fax: 01491 682425
E-mail: FineFood@aol.com
Mail order only; membership fee deducted from first order; selections include British sausages and smoked goods, along with cheese and breads

Harrods Food Hall
87-135 Brompton Road
London SW1X 7XL
Tel: 0171 730 1234
Fax: 0171 225 6667
Mail order and retail; wide range of British and international groceries and fresh produce

Harvey Nichols Food Hall
109-125 Knightsbridge
London SW3 1EF
Tel: 0171 235 5000
Fax: 0171 235 5020
Mail order and retail; wide range of British and international groceries and fresh produce

House of Albert Roux
229 Ebury Street
London SW1W 8UT
Tel: 0171 730 3037
Fax: 0171 823 5043
Mail order and retail; specialises in French breads and cheeses, along with oils, vinegars and condiments

Selfridges Food Hall
400 Oxford Street
London W1A 1AB
Tel: 0171 629 1234
Fax: 0171 491 1880
Mail order and retail; wide range of British and international groceries and fresh produce, with good cheese department

ASIAN SPECIALITIES

Chiman's
Trifolau
High Street
Stockbridge
Hampshire SO20 6EU
Tel: 01264 811161
Mail order only; Asian spice mixtures

Curry Club Direct
PO Box 109
Brignorth
Shropshire WV16 4WE
Tel/fax: 01746 761211
E-mail: curry.direct@dial.pipex.com
Mail order only

BREADS

See also General Specialist Ingredients, left

& Clarke's
122 Kensington Church Street
London W8 4BH
Tel: 0171 229 2190
Primarily retail, but non-perishable goods can be ordered by mail; one of London's most popular bread shops; also good for cheeses, oils, vinegars, condiments and seasonal produce

De Gustibus
Unit 7-10
Fritzharrys Trading Estate
Wootton Road
Abingdon
Oxfordshire OX14 1JD
Tel: 01235 555777
Fax: 01235 537999
Mail order and retail; sourdough and rye breads are specialities

De Gustibus
53 Blandford St
London W1H 5RM
Tel/Fax: 0171 486 6608
Mail order and retail

Village Bakery
Melmerby
Cumbria CA10 1HE
Tel: 01768 881515
Fax: 01768 881848
Mail order and retail; range includes sourdough breads

CHEESES

See also General Specialist Ingredients, left

Abergavenny Fine Foods
4 Castle Meadows Park
Abergavenny
Gwent NP7 7RZ
Tel: 01873 850001
Fax: 01873 850002
Mail order and retail; Welsh cheeses are specialities

Colston Bassett Dairy
Harby Lane
Colston Bassett
Nottinghamshire NG12 3FN
Tel/Fax: 019049 81322
Mail order and retail; makers of acclaimed blue cheese

Ian Mellis, the
  Cheesemonger
30a Victoria Street
Edinburgh EH11 2JN
Tel/Fax: 0131 226 6215
*Mail order and retail; British
  and international cheeses*

Jeroboams
96 Holland Park Ave
London W11 3RB
Tel: 0171 727 9792
Fax: 0171 792 3672
*Mail order and retail; British
  and international cheeses,
  along with oils, vinegars and
  condiments*

Neals Yard Dairy Mail Order
6 Park Street
Borough Market
London SE1 9AB
Tel: 0171 403 9544
Fax: 0171 378 0400
*Mail order from this location;
  retail shop is at Neals Yard,
  Covent Garden, London;
  good British farmhouse
  cheeses, along with olives, oils
  and condiments*

The Teddington Cheese
42 Station Road
Teddington
Middlesex TW11 9AA
Tel: 0181 977 6868
Fax: 0181 977 2318
*Mail order and retail; British
  and international cheeses*

COOKING EQUIPMENT

Lakeland Limited
Alexandra Buildings
Windermere
Cumbria LA23 1BQ
Tel: 01539 488100
Fax: 01539 488300

*Mail order and retail; other
  shops throughout the country*

Nisbets
Freepost BS4675
Bristol
Avon BS2 OYZ
Tel: 01454 855525
Fax: 01454 855565
*Mail order; clothing and chef's
  equipment*

NUTS AND DRIED FRUITS

*See also General Specialist
  Ingredients, p. 124*

Julian Graves Ltd.
Unit 4, The Rye Market
Stourbridge
West Midlands DY8 1HJ
Tel: 01384 442206
Fax: 01384 297707
*Mail order and retail; other
  retail outlets throughout
  the UK*

Meg Game
Oldbury Farmhouse
Ightham
Kent TN15 9DE
Tel: 01732 882397
*Mail order, or pick your own
  until the end of September:
  Kentish cob nuts*

OILS, VINEGARS AND CONDIMENTS

*See also General Specialist
  Ingredients, p. 124*

Carluccio's
28A Neal Atreet
Covent Garden
London WC2H 9PS
Tel: 0171 240 1487
Fax: 0171 497 1361

*Mail order for non-perishable
  items and retail; offers a wide
  range of Italian oils, vinegars
  and bottled sauces; good
  selection of prime vegetables,
  herbs and wild mushrooms
  in season*

Gordon's Condiments
Gordon House
Little Mead Industrial Estate
Cranleigh
Surrey GU6 8ND
Tel: 01483 267707
Fax: 01483 267783
*Mail order; products sold by
  retail outlets throughout
  the UK*

Les Fines Herbes
8 St Mary's Hill
Stamford
Lincolnshire PE9 2DP
Tel: 01780 757381
*Mail order and retail; herb-
  and flower-flavoured
  vinegars*

Wiltshire Tracklements
Sherston
Wiltshire SN16 0XN
Tel: 01666 840851
Fax: 01666 840022
*Mail order only; additive-free
  mustards and salad dressings;
  also sold by retail outlets
  throughout the UK*

Womersley Crafts & Herbs
Womersley Hall
Womersley
Doncaster
Yorkshire DN6 9BH
Tel: 01977 620294
*Mail order and retail (limited
  hours – telephone ahead);
  herb- and flower-flavoured
  vinegars*

Valvona & Crolla
19 Elm Row
Edinburgh EH7 4AA
Tel: 0131 556 6066
Fax: 0131 556 1668
*Mail order and retail; one of
  Scotland's most popular
  delicatessens offers a wide
  range of Italian oils and
  vinegars, along with Italian
  and international cheeses
  and sausages; good
  selection of fresh salad
  ingredients (retail only)*

SAUSAGES AND MEATS

*See also General Specialist
  Ingredients, p. 124*

Blas ar Fwyd
25 Heol yr Orsaf
Llanrwst
Gwynedd LL26 0BT
Tel: 01492 640215
Fax: 01492 642215
*Mail order and retail; also sells
  Welsh cheeses*

Bryan Pickering
30 The Street
Old Costessey
Norwich
Norfolk NR8 5DB
Tel: 01603 742002
Fax: 01603 743352
*Mail order and retail; ring for a list
  of products; discounts on orders
  weighing 2.3 and 4.5kg (5 and
  10lb)*

Eastbrook Farm Organic
  Meat
50 High Street
Shrivenham
Oxfordshire SN6 8AA
Tel: 01793 782211

Index